NOTES FROM THE AIR

Also by JOHN ASHBERY

Poetry

JOHN ASHBERY

Notes from the Air

SELECTED LATER POEMS

ecco

An Imprint of HarperCollinsPublishers

HarperCollins books may be purchased for educational, business, or sales promotional use. For information please write: Special Markets Department, HarperCollins Publishers, 10 East 53rd Street, New York, NY 10022.

A hardcover edition of this book was published in 2007 by Ecco, an imprint of HarperCollinsPublishers.

FIRST ECCO PAPERBACK PUBLISHED 2008.

Library of Congress Cataloging-in-Publication Data is available upon request.

ISBN 978-0-06-136718-2

08 09 10 11 12 ID/RRD 10 9 8 7 6 5 4 3 2 1

FOR DAVID

CONTENTS

from CHINESE WHISPERS   *(2002)*

from WHERE SHALL I WANDER *(2005)*

ACKNOWLEDGMENTS

The author gratefully acknowledges the publications in which the poems in this book first appeared, sometimes in slightly different form:

American Poetry Review, Annals of Scholarship, Antaeus, Arshile, Bad Henry Review, Bard Papers, Birthday Boy: A Present for Lee Harwood, Black Warrior Review, Boston Review, Boulevard, Broadway 2, The Bulletin, Café Review, Carcanet 2000: A Commonplace Book, Chelsea, Colorado Review, Combo, Conjunctions, Cover, Cuz, Denver Quarterly, The Drawing Center's Line Reading: An Anthology 2000–2001, Epoch, Fence, Forbes, A Garland for Stephen Spender, The Germ, Gold Coast, Grand Street, Green Mountains Review, Harvard Advocate, Harvard Book Review, Harvard Review, The Hat, Hodos, Hotel Amerika, Iowa Review, Jacket, Joe Soap's Canoe, jubilat, Kenyon Review, Kunapipi, Lingo, London Quarterly, London Review of Books, Michigan Quarterly Review, Modern Painters, Mudfish, murmur, Nest, New American Writing, New Republic, New York Review of Books, The New York Times, The New Yorker, Numbers, o·blēk, Occident, L'Oeil de Boeuf, Ohio Review, On Paper, Painted Bride Quarterly, Paris Review, Partisan Review, PN Review, Poetry, Poetry New York, Poetry Review (UK), The Poker, Princeton Library Chronicle, Privates, Raritan, riverrun, St. Mark's Newsletter, Salt, Scripsi, Shenandoah, Shiny, Soho Square, Southwest Review, Stand, Sulfur, Temblor, The Times Literary Supplement, Verse, Voices, Walker Art Center Bridge Book, Whitney Museum 1995 Biennial Catalogue, Writing for Bernadette [Mayer], *The World, Yale Review,* and fine art editions by the Kaldewey Press (with Jonathan Lasker) and Z Press (with Elizabeth Murray).

"[untitled]" was commissioned by Siah Armajani for use in his Irene Hixon Whitney Bridge at the Walker Arts Center, Minneapolis, Minnesota.

This ornament is used to indicate a stanza break lost in pagination:

[. . .]

from APRIL GALLEONS

(1987)

VETIVER

Ages passed slowly, like a load of hay,
As the flowers recited their lines
And pike stirred at the bottom of the pond.
The pen was cool to the touch.
The staircase swept upward
Through fragmented garlands, keeping the melancholy
Already distilled in letters of the alphabet.

It would be time for winter now, its spun-sugar
Palaces and also lines of care
At the mouth, pink smudges on the forehead and cheeks,
The color once known as "ashes of roses."
How many snakes and lizards shed their skins
For time to be passing on like this,
Sinking deeper in the sand as it wound toward
The conclusion. It had all been working so well and now,
Well, it just kind of came apart in the hand
As a change is voiced, sharp
As a fishhook in the throat, and decorative tears flowed
Past us into a basin called infinity.

    [. . .]

There was no charge for anything, the gates
Had been left open intentionally.
Don't follow, you can have whatever it is.
And in some room someone examines his youth,
Finds it dry and hollow, porous to the touch.
O keep me with you, unless the outdoors
Embraces both of us, unites us, unless
The birdcatchers put away their twigs,
The fishermen haul in their sleek empty nets
And others become part of the immense crowd
Around this bonfire, a situation
That has come to mean us to us, and the crying
In the leaves is saved, the last silver drops.

RIDDLE ME

Rainy days are best,
There is some permanence in the angle
That things make with the ground;
In not taking off after apologies.
   The speedometer's at sundown.

Even as they spoke the sun was beginning to disappear behind a cloud.
All right so it's better to have vague outlines
But wrapped, tightly, around one's mood
Of something like vengeful joy. And in the wood
   It's all the same too.

I think I liked you better when I seldom knew you.
But lovers are like hermits or cats: They
Don't know when to come in, to stop
Breaking off twigs for dinner.
   In the little station I waited for you

And shall, what with all the interest
I bear toward plans of yours and the future
Of stars it makes me thirsty
Just to go down on my knees looking
   In the sawdust for joy.

June and the nippers will scarcely look our way.
And be bold then it's then
This cloud imagines us and all that our story
Was ever going to be, and we catch up
   To ourselves, but they are the selves of others.
     [. . .]

And with it all the city starts to live
As a place where one can believe in moving
To a particular name and be there, and then
It's more action falling back refreshed into death.
 We can survive the storms, wearing us

Like rainbow hats, afraid to retrace steps
To the past that was only recently ours,
Afraid of finding a party there.
O in all your life were you ever teased
 Like this, and it became your mind?

Where still some saunter on the bank in mixed
Plum shade and weary sun, resigned
To the installations on the opposite bank, we mix
Breathless greetings and tears and lately taste
 The precious supplies.

A MOOD OF QUIET BEAUTY

The evening light was like honey in the trees
When you left me and walked to the end of the street
Where the sunset abruptly ended.
The wedding-cake drawbridge lowered itself
To the fragile forget-me-not flower.
You climbed aboard.

Burnt horizons suddenly paved with golden stones,
Dreams I had, including suicide,
Puff out the hot-air balloon now.
It is bursting, it is about to burst
With something invisible
Just during the days.
We hear, and sometimes learn,
Pressing so close

And fetch the blood down, and things like that.
Museums then became generous, they live in our breath.

FINNISH RHAPSODY

He managed the shower, coped with the small spattering drops,
Then rubbed himself dry with a towel, wiped the living organism.
Day extended its long promise, light swept through his refuge.
But it was time for business, back to the old routine.

Many there are, a crowd exists at present,
For whom the daily forgetting, to whom the diurnal plunge
Truncates the spadelike shadows, chops off the blades of darkness,
To be rescued, to be guided into a state of something like security.
Yet it falls off for others; for some, however, it drops from sight:
The millers, winnowers of wheat,
Dusted with snow-white flour, glazed with farinaceous powder,
Like Pierrot, like the white clown of chamber music;
The leggy mannequins, models slender and tall;
The sad children, the disappointed kids.

And for these few, to this small group
Forgetting means remembering the ranks, oblivion is recalling the rows
Of flowers each autumn and spring; of blooms in the fall and early summer.
But those traveling by car, those nosing the vehicle out into the crowded highway
And at the posts of evening, the tall poles of declining day,
Returning satisfied, their objective accomplished,
Note neither mystery nor alarm, see no strangeness or cause for fright.
And these run the greatest risk at work, are endangered by their employment
Seeing there can be no rewards later, no guerdon save in the present:
Strong and severe punishment, *peine forte et dure,*
Or comfort and relaxation, coziness and tranquillity.

Don't fix it if it works, tinker not with that which runs apace,
Otherwise the wind might get it, the breeze waft it away.
There is no time for anything like chance, no spare moment for the aleatory,
Because the closing of our day is business, the bottom line already here.

One wonders what roadblocks were set up for, we question barricades:
Is it the better to time, jot down the performance time of
Anything irregular, all that doesn't fit the preconceived mold
Of our tentative offerings and withdrawals, our hesitant giving and taking back?
For those who perform correctly, for the accurate, painstaking ones
Do accomplish their business, get the job done,
And are seldom seen again, and are rarely glimpsed after that.
That there are a few more black carriages, more somber chariots
For some minutes, over a brief period,
Signifies business as usual, means everything is OK,
That the careful have gone to their reward, the capable disappeared
And boobies, or nincompoops, numskulls and sapheads,
Persist, faced with eventual destruction; endure to be confronted with annihilation
    someday.

The one who runs little, he who barely trips along
Knows how short the day is, how few the hours of light.
Distractions can't wrench him, preoccupations forcibly remove him
From the heap of things, the pile of this and that:
Tepid dreams and mostly worthless; lukewarm fancies, the majority of them unprofitable.
Yet it is from these that the light, from the ones present here that luminosity
Sifts and breaks, subsides and falls asunder.
And it will be but half-strange, really be only semi-bizarre
When the tall poems of the world, the towering earthbound poetic utterances
Invade the street of our dialect, penetrate the avenue of our patois,
Bringing fresh power and new knowledge, transporting virgin might and up-to-date
    enlightenment
To this place of honest thirst, to this satisfyingly parched here and now,
Since all things congregate, because everything assembles
In front of him, before the one
Who need only sit and tie his shoelace, who should remain seated, knotting the metal-
    tipped cord

For it to happen right, to enable it to come correctly into being
As moments, then years; minutes, afterwards ages
Suck up the common strength, absorb the everyday power
And afterwards live on, satisfied; persist, later to be a source of gratification,
But perhaps only to oneself, haply to one's sole identity.

ALONE IN THE LUMBER BUSINESS

It's still too early to make concessions.
Meanwhile the long night glided on,
Intent on some adventure of its own, like a dog
Dreaming of a bone. But under the coat of burrs

Lay the stones, and they were awake, desire
Still shriveled in the bud, but they were there,
Soon to be on fire. As the tree beautifies itself
Over a period of several months, all things

Take up their abode in the questions it asks,
And don't even dream of them, perhaps. Poor, misguided pilgrim,
It says, overtaken by every new tempest
That comes along, your cloak, the half you kept, caked with mud.

Life, it thinks, is like growing up
Entrusted to the sole care of a French governess,
Never knowing anything about your parents,
As lights come on in the city far across the bay.

Then it's suddenly an orgy of name-giving,
Of hyphenated names, names with "Dr." attached to them,
The flowers waiting to be named, the days
Of the month, and so on. And the medicines.

And it's like not being grown up anymore,
Like being a fifty-seven-year-old child or something,
The secret having leaked out again. No
Name quite sticks. Wine and cider

    [. . .]

Taste like Chinese-restaurant tea.
One has cobbled a kind of life together,
The cloud and outlines of the sod
Still glowing, longing to touch you with the fire

That shapes us, then replaces us on the shelf.
It's safe around here though. Something
In the darkness understands, tries to make up for it all.
But it's like a new disease, a resistant strain.

Where were you when it was all happening?
Night is full of kindred spirits now,
Voices, photos of loved ones, faces
Out of the newspaper, eager smiles blown like leaves

Before they become fungus. No time to give credit
Where it is due, though actions, as before,
Speak louder than words. To dot the i's,
Cross the t's and tie everything up

In a loose bundle stamped "not wanted on the voyage."
There were flowers in a garden once,
Monkey business, shenanigans. But it all
Gets towered over. There would be no point

In replying to the finer queries, since we live
In our large, square, open landscape. The bridge
Of fools once crossed, there are adjustments to be made.
But you have to settle in to looking at these things.

VAUCANSON

It was snowing as he wrote.
In the gray room he felt relaxed and singular,
But no one, of course, ever trusts these moods.

There had to be understanding to it.
Why, though? That always happens anyway,
And who gets the credit for it? Not what is understood,
Presumably, and it diminishes us
In our getting to know it

As trees come to know a storm
Until it passes and light falls anew
Unevenly, on all the muttering kinship:
Things with things, persons with objects,
Ideas with people or ideas.

It hurts, this wanting to give a dimension
To life, when life is precisely that dimension.
We are creatures, therefore we walk and talk
And people come up to us, or listen
And then move away.

Music fills the spaces
Where figures are pulled to the edges,
And it can only say something.

Sinews are loosened then,
The mind begins to think good thoughts.
Ah, this sun must be good:
It's warming again,
Doing a number, completing its trilogy.
Life must be back there. You hid it

So no one would find it
And now you can't remember where.

But if one were to invent being a child again
It might just come close enough to being a living relic
To save this thing, save it from embarrassment
By ringing down the curtain,

And for a few seconds no one would notice.
The ending would seem perfect.
No feelings to dismay,
No tragic sleep to wake from in a fit
Of passionate guilt, only the warm sunlight
That slides easily down shoulders
To the soft, melting heart.

SOMEONE YOU HAVE SEEN BEFORE

It was a night for listening to Corelli, Geminiani
Or Manfredini. The tables had been set with beautiful white cloths
And bouquets of flowers. Outside the big glass windows
The rain drilled mercilessly into the rock garden, which made light
Of the whole thing. Both business and entertainment waited
With parted lips, because so much new way of being
With one's emotion and keeping track of it at the same time
Had been silently expressed. Even the waiters were happy.

It was an example of how much one can grow lustily
Without fracturing the shell of coziness that surrounds us,
And all things as well. "We spend so much time
Trying to convince ourselves we're happy that we don't recognize
The real thing when it comes along," the Disney official said.
He's got a point, you must admit. If we followed nature
More closely we'd realize that, I mean really getting your face pressed
Into the muck and indecision of it. Then it's as if
We grew out of our happiness, not the other way round, as is
Commonly supposed. We're the characters in its novel,
And anybody who doubts that need only look out of the window
Past his or her own reflection, to the bright, patterned,
Timeless unofficial truth hanging around out there,
Waiting for the signal to be galvanized into a crowd scene,
Joyful or threatening, it doesn't matter, so long as we know
It's inside, here with us.

But people do change in life,
As well as in fiction. And what happens then? Is it because we think nobody's
Listening that one day it comes, the urge to delete yourself,
"Take yourself out," as they say? As though this could matter
Even to the concerned ones who crowd around,
Expressions of lightness and peace on their faces,

In which you play no part perhaps, but even so
Their happiness is for you, it's your birthday, and even
When the balloons and fudge get tangled with extraneous
Good wishes from everywhere, it is, I believe, made to order
For your questioning stance and that impression
Left on the inside of your pleasure by some bivalve
With which you have been identified. Sure,
Nothing is ever perfect enough, but that's part of how it fits
The mixed bag
Of leftover character traits that used to be part of you
Before the change was performed
And of all those acquaintances bursting with vigor and
Humor, as though they wanted to call you down
Into closeness, not for being close, or snug, or whatever,
But because they believe you were made to fit this unique
And valuable situation whose lid is rising, totally
Into the morning-glory-colored future. Remember, don't throw away
The quadrant of unused situations just because they're here:
They may not always be, and you haven't finished looking
Through them all yet. So much that happens happens in small ways
That someone was going to get around to tabulate, and then never did,
Yet it all bespeaks freshness, clarity and an even motor drive
To coax us out of sleep and start us wondering what the new round
Of impressions and salutations is going to leave in its wake
This time. And the form, the precepts, are yours to dispose of as you will,
As the ocean makes grasses, and in doing so refurbishes a lighthouse
On a distant hill, or else lets the whole picture slip into foam.

OSTENSIBLY

One might like to rest or read,
Take walks, celebrate the kitchen table,
Pat the dog absentmindedly, meanwhile
Thinking gloomy thoughts—so many separate
Ways of doing, one is uncertain
How the future is going to handle this.
Will it reveal itself again,
Or only in the artificial calm
Of one person's resolve to do better
Yet strike a harder bargain,
Next time?

Gardeners cannot make the world
Nor witches undo it, yet
The mad doctor is secure
In his thick-walled laboratory,
Behind evergreen borders black now
Against the snow, precise as stocking seams
Pulled straight again. There is never
Any news from that side.

A rigidity that may well be permanent
Seems to have taken over. The pendulum
Is stilled; the rush
Of season into season ostensibly incomplete.
A perverse order has been laid
There at the joint where the year branches
Into artifice one way, into a votive
Lassitude the other way, but that is stalled:
An old discolored snapshot
That soon fades away.

    [. . .]

And so there is no spectator
And no agent to cry Enough,
That the battle chime is stilled,
The defeated memory gracious as flowers
And therefore also permanent in its way—
I mean they endure, are always around,
And even when they are not, their names are,
A fortified dose of the solid,
Livable adventure.

And from growing dim, the coals
Fall alight. There are two ways to be.
You must try getting up from the table
And sitting down relaxed in another country
Wearing red suspenders
Toward one's own space and time.

BECALMED ON STRANGE WATERS

In the presence of both, each mistook
The other's sincerity for an elaborate plot.
And perhaps something like that did occur—who knows?
There was some hostility, hostility
In the way they talked together
As the drops of warm liquor went down.

In the sky's sensual pout, the crazy kindness
Of statues, the scraps of leaves still blowing around
Self-importantly after winter was well under way;
In the closed greeting, the firm handclasp,
Was matter enough for one or more dreams,
Even bad ones, but certainly some getting grim
Around the edges. We smile at these,

Thinking them matter for a child's euphuistic
Tale of what goes on in the morning,
After everyone but the cat has left. But can you
See otherwise? O ecstatic
Receiver of what's there to be received,
How we belabor thee, how much better
To wait and to prepare our waiting
For the grand rush, the mass of detail
Still compacted in the excitement that lies ahead,
Like a Japanese paper flower.

THE BIG CLOUD

For ages man has labored to put his dreams in order. Look at the result.
Once an idea like the correct time is elucidated
It must fade or spread. Decay, under the old tree, is noted.
That's why we frame them, try to keep them on a wall,
Though it is decreed that the companionable
Trooping down to be with us, to partly become us
Must continue for them and us to flourish:
The obliging feathers once parted,
The object of our sight, grass, just sits there
Like an empty flowerpot on a windowsill.

And a new dream gets us involved further
In that closeness. Yes, I knew there
Were sheets of tulips and pointed leaves
To screen us from each other, what we were all about,
And an announcement made against the lukewarm atmosphere of the room
To all that did or did not belong in it.

Finally, it seems, they have scattered.
Not one specimen was actually available.
And they call this peace, living our lives, and so on.
To point the finger of blame—ah, surely, at no one?
Each system trickles out into its set number of instances.
Poles strike bottom,
Finding the river sludge good to them, a companionable feeling.
Meetings occur under grotesquely overscaled arcades,
Last words are uttered, and first love
Ascends to its truly majestic position unimpaired.

[. . .]

Letters were strewn across the floor,
Singing the joyful song of how no one was ever going to read them.
Trees and wisteria rose and sank in the breeze,
And laughter danced in the dim fields beyond the schoolhouse:
It was existence again in all its tautness,
Playing its adolescent joke, its pictures
Teasing our notion of fragility with their monumental permanence.
But life was never the same again. Something faltered,
Something went away.

SOME MONEY

I said I am awkward.
I said we make fools of our lives
For a little money and a coat.
The great tree, once grown, passes over.
I said you can catch all kinds of weird activities.

Meanwhile the child disturbs you.
You are never asked back with its dog
And the fishing pole leans against the steps.
Why have all the windows darkened?
The laurel burned its image into the sky like smoke?

All was gold and shiny in the queen's parlor.
In the pigsty outside it was winter however
With one headache after another
Leading to the blasted bush
On which a felt hat was stuck
Closer to the image of you, of how it feels.
The dogs were in time for no luck.
The lobster shouted how it was long ago
No pen mightier than this said the object
As though to ward off a step
To kiss my sweetheart in the narrow alley
Before it was wartime and the cold ended
On that note.

WET ARE THE BOARDS

Not liking what life has in it,
"It's probably dead, whatever it is,"
You said, and turned, and thought
Of one spot on the ground, what it means to all of us
Passing through the earth. And the reasonable, filleted
Nymph of the fashions of the air points to that too:
"No need to be deprived. We are all
Friends here,
And whatever it takes to get us out of the mess we're in
One of us has."

Fair enough, and the spirited bulk,
The work of a local architect, knows how to detach itself
From the little puffs issuing from the mouths of the four winds,
Yet not too much, and be honest
While still remaining noble and sedate.
The tepees on the front lawn
Of the governor's palace became a fixture there
And were cast in stone after the originals rotted away.
Fish tanks glinted from within the varnished
Halls of jurisprudence and it was possible to save
The friezes, of Merovingian thrust,
And so much else made to please the senses:
Like a plum tree dripping brilliants
On a round dirt bed, and all the stories of the ducks.
Now if only I were a noncombatant—
Which brings us back to the others: philosophers,
Pedants, and criminals intent on enjoying the public view—
Is it just another panorama?
For we none of us
Can determine strictly what they are thinking,
Even the one we walk arm in arm with

Through the darkling purple air of spring, so when it comes
Time to depart our good-byes will read automatically true or false
According to what has gone before.
And that loneliness will accompany us
On the far side of parting, when what we dream, we read.
No hand is outstretched
Through the bored gloom unless more thinking wants to take us elsewhere
Into space that seems changed by luck or just by time hanging around,
And the mystery of the family that bore you
Into the race that is, reversing the story

So that the end showed through the paper as the beginning
And all children were nice again.
Pause again at the scenery
Whirling to destroy itself, and what a different face
It wears when order smiles, as I think it
Does here. Our costumes
Must never be folded and put back into the trunk again,
Or someone too young for the part is going to step up
And say, "Listen, I made it. It's mine,"
In a November twilight when the frost is creeping over you
As surely as waves across a beach, since no chill is complete
Without our unique participation. And when you walk away
You might reflect that this is an aspect
In which all of the cores and seeds are visible,
That it's a matter of not choosing to see.

OFFSHORE BREEZE

Perhaps I have merely forgotten,
Perhaps it really was like you say.
How can I know?
While life grows increasingly mysterious and dangerous
With nobody else really visible,
And I am alone and quiet
Like the grass this day of no wind
And sizzling knowledge.
The leaves fall, fall off and burn.

At least one can nap until the Day of Judgment—
Or can one? Be careful what you say, the perturbed
Flock shifts and retreats
In a colorful equation of long standing.
No one knew what microorganisms
Were metamorphosing. I like you
Because it's all I *can* do.

What happens is you get the unreconstructed story,
An offshore breeze pushing one gently away,
Not far away. And the leggings of those meeting to
See about it are a sunset,
Brilliant and disordered, and sharp
As a word held in the mouth too long.
And he spat out the pit.

isn't really a storm of course because unlike most storms it isn't one till it's over and people go outside and say will you look at that. And by then it's of course starting to collapse. Diamond rubble, all galled glitter, heaps of this and that in corners and beside posts where the draft has left them—are you sure it's this you were waiting for while the storm—the real one—pressed it all into the earth to emphasize a point that melts away as fast as another idea enters the chain of them in the conversation about earth and sky and woods and how you should be good to your parents and not cheat at cards. The summer's almost over it seems to say. Did I say summer I meant to say winter it seems to say. You know when nature really has to claw like this to get her effects that something's not ripe or nice, i.e., the winter, our favorite of the seasons, the one that goes by quickest although you almost never hear anyone say, I wonder where the winter has gone. But anyone engaged in the business of swapping purity for depth will understand what I mean. So we all eyeball it, agog, for a while. And soon our attention is trapped by news from the cities, by what comes over the wireless—*heated,* and alight. How natural then to retreat into what we have been doing, trying to capture the old songs, the idiot games whose rules have been forgotten. "Here we go looby, looby." And the exact name of the season that stings like a needle made of frozen mercury falls through the infinitesimal hole in our consciousness, to plummet hundreds of leagues into the sea and vanish in a perpetual descent toward the ocean floor, whatever and wherever that may be, and the great undersea storms and cataclysms will leave no trace on the seismographs each of us wears in the guise of a head.

To do that, though—get up and out from under the pile of required reading such as obituary notices of the near-great—"He first gained employment as a schoolmaster in his native Northamptonshire. Of his legendary wit, no trace remains"—is something that will go unthought of until another day. Sure we know that the government and the president want it. But we know just as surely that until the actual slippage occurs, the actual moment of uncertainty by two or more of the plates or tectons that comprise the earth's crust, nobody is ever going to be moved to the point of action. You might as well call it a night, go to sleep under a bushel basket. For the probability of that moment occurring is next to nil. I mean it will probably never happen and if it does, chances are we won't be around to witness any of it.

The warp, the woof. (What, actually, are they? Never mind, save that for another time when the old guy's gotten a bit more soused.) Or the actual strings of words on the two pages of a book, like "I was reading this novel, I think the author was associated with the Kailyard School." What's that? Wait, though—I think I know. What I really want to know is how will this affect me, make me better in the future? Maybe make me a better conversationalist? But nobody I know ever talks about the Kailyard School, at least not at the dinner parties I go to. What, then? Will it be that having accomplished the tale of this reading there will only be about seven million more books to go, and that's something, or is it more the act of reading something, of being communicated to by an author and thus having one's ideas displaced like the water that pebbles placed by the stork's beak slowly force out of the beaker—*beaker?* do you suppose? No, I wasn't suggesting anything like that. I want to cut out of this conversation or discourse. Why? Because it doesn't seem to be leading anywhere. Besides it could compromise me when the results become known, and by results I mean the slightest ripple that occurs as when the breeze lifts a corner of the vast torpid flag drooping at its standard, like the hairline crack in the milk-white china of the sky, that indicates something is off, something less likable than the situation a few moments before has assumed its place in the preordained hierarchy of things. Something like the leaves of this plant with their veins that almost look parallel though they are radiating from their centers of course.

It's odd about things like plants. Today I found a rose in full bloom in the wreck of the garden, all the living color and sentience but also the sententiousness drained out of it. What remained was like a small flower in the woods, too pale and sickly to notice. No, sickly isn't the right word, the thing was normal and healthy by its own standards, and thriving merrily along its allotted path toward death. Only we hold it up to some real and abject notion of what a living organism ought to be and paint it as a scarecrow that frightens birds away (presumably) but isn't able to frighten itself away. Oh, no, it's far too clever for that! But our flower, the one we saw, really had no need of us to justify its blooming where it did. So we ought to think about our own position on the path. Will it ever be anything more than that of pebble? I wonder. And they scratch, some of them feverishly, at whatever meaning it might be supposed to yield up, of course expiring as it does so. But our rose gains its distinction just by being stuck there as though by the distracted hand of a caterer putting the finishing touch on some grand floral display for a society wedding that will be over in a few minutes, a season not of its own naming. Why appear at a time when the idea of a flower can make no sense, not even in its isolation? It's just that nature forces us into odd positions and then sits back to hear us squawk but may, indeed, derive no comfort or pleasure from this. And as I lifted it gently I saw that it was doing what it was supposed to do—miming freshness tracked by pathos. What more do you want? it seemed to say. Leave me in this desert . . .

As I straightened my footsteps to accommodate the narrow path that has been chosen for me I begin to cringe at the notion that I can never be assimilated here, no, not like the rose blooming grotesquely out of season even, but must always consider the sharp edges of the slender stones set upright in the earth, to be my guide and commentator, on this path. I was talking to some of the others about it. But if it didn't matter then, it matters now, now that I begin to get my bearings in this gloom and see how I could improve on the distraught situation all around me, in the darkness and tarnished earth. Yet who will save me from myself if they can't? I can't, certainly, yet I tell myself it all seems like fun and will work out in the end. I expect I will be asked a question I can answer and then be handed a big prize. They're working on it.

So the sunlit snow slips daintily down the waterway to the open sea, the car with its driver along the looping drives that bisect suburbs and then flatten out through towns that are partly rural though with some suburban characteristics. Only I stay here alone, waiting for it to reach the point of cohesion. Or maybe I'm not alone, maybe there are other me's, but in that case the cohesion may have happened already and we are no wiser for it, despite being positioned around to comment on it like statues around a view. The dry illumination that results from that will not help us, it will always be as though we had never happened, ornaments on a structure whose mass remains invisible or illegible.

October 28. Three more days till November. I expect this to happen in a soft explosion of powdery light, dull and nameless, though not without a sense of humor in its crevices, where darkness still lives and enjoys going about its business. There are too many stones to make it interesting to hobble from one to another. Perhaps in a few days . . . Maybe by the time I finish the course I am taking, if sirens don't dislodge me from this pure and valid niche. I feel that this season is being pulled over my head like a dress, difficult to spot the dirt in its mauve and brick traceries. I am being taken out into the country. Trees flash past. All is perhaps for the best then since I am going, and they are going with us, with us as we go. The past is only a pond. The present is a lake of grass. Between your two futures, yours and his, numbing twigs chart the pattern of lifeless chatter in shut-down night, starstruck the magnitudes that would make us theirs, too cold to matter to themselves, let us be off anywhere, to Alaska, to Arizona. I am fishing for compliments. The afternoon lasts forever.

APRIL GALLEONS

Something *was* burning. And besides,
At the far end of the room a discredited waltz
Was alive and reciting tales of the conquerors
And their lilies—is all of life thus
A tepid housewarming? And where do the scraps
Of meaning come from? Obviously,
It was time to be off, in another
Direction, toward marshlands and cold, scrolled
Names of cities that sounded as though they existed,
But never had. I could see the scow
Like a nail file pointed at the pleasures
Of the great open sea, that it would stop for me,
That you and I should sample the disjointedness
Of a far-from-level deck, and then return, some day,
Through the torn orange veils of an early evening
That will know our names only in a different
Pronunciation, and then, and only then,
Might the profit-taking of spring arrive
In due course, as one says, with the gesture
Of a bird taking off for some presumably
Better location, though not major, perhaps,
In the sense that a winged guitar would be major
If we had one. And all trees seemed to exist.

Then there was a shorter day with dank
Tapestries streaming initials of all the previous owners
To warn us into silence and waiting. Would the mouse
Know us now, and if so, how far would propinquity
Admit discussion of the difference: crumb or other
Less perceptible boon? It was all going
To be scattered anyway, as far from one's wish
As the root of the tree from the center of the earth

From which it nonetheless issued in time to
Inform us of happy blossoms and tomorrow's
Festival of the vines. Just being under them
Sometimes makes you wonder how much you know
And then you wake up and you know, but not
How much. In intervals in the twilight notes from an
Untuned mandolin seem to coexist with their
Question and the no less urgent reply. Come
To look at us but not too near or its familiarity
Will vanish in a thunderclap and the beggar-girl,
String-haired and incomprehensibly weeping, will
Be all that is left of the golden age, our
Golden age, and no longer will the swarms
Issue forth at dawn to return in a rain of mild
Powder at night removing us from our boring and
Unsatisfactory honesty with tales of colored cities,
Of how the mist built there, and what were the
Directions the lepers were taking
To avoid these eyes, the old eyes of love.

from **FLOW CHART**

[section V *of* VI*]*

(1991)

V.

Nothing is required of you, yet all must render an accounting.
I said I was out hunting in the forest. How can it be that a man
can sup his fill, and still all around him find emptiness and drowsiness,
if he must go to the grave this way, unattended? Yet certainly
there are some bright spots, and when you listen to the laughter
in the middle of these it makes for more than a cosmetic truth, an invitation
to chivalry ringed by the dump fires of our deliberate civilization that has
got some things going for it—that invented neighborliness, for instance?
Then the paltry painted guest goes away, leaving behind the screed
she omitted to read. What's in it for us? Out of this school was sucked a philosophy
that didn't impel to action. A back-burner sort of thing. But if people had but
kept track of it that would have been something, someone could have framed
a memorandum. But they quickly find out what the traffic will bear
and are soon asleep in the midst of it, and the next call to action is considered passé
and no one will believe you represent the right cause. A piece of webbing
is nailed to the ground; ring-grass
invades its orient extremity; even these criteria have to be put away
until later. The hangar gets unbearably hot and very smelly.
Meanwhile the new green cascades silently and as it were invisibly.
Something has been said. You're right about that. But no two people
can agree on what it means, as though we were sounding boards
for each childish attempt at wireless communication the gods can invent,
and so return to our refectory. But I didn't know but what if I
didn't hang around a little longer the thrust
would be vouchsafed to *me* this time and of course as its public
repository I would use it to further the interests of all men and women,
not just some. And it left the same message. It was as though
it never got my previous message. Sure, I'm still not yet compromised
but there was so much in those fierce screens that ought to have lived
as an example to conceal more and then to have it break out of control and be put
down again if ever I could will myself to wish it, instead of lingering
like a daisy on muck. Take out my tricycle for a spin and return it

before anyone missed me. Yet, as I said, I didn't know. The old men at the urinal
spat, not wanting word to get out. All my links with a certain past were severed.
I let fall the book I had been reading, *The Radiator Girls at Strapontin Lodge*,
as so much gift to the giver of idiosyncrasies which when adopted
sift down like bran on rutted earth to accumulate
in whorls, and I thought how I could give no account
of these latest days. It was as though I had gone through a bout of amnesia.
Now I was ready to put the gloves on again, but wasn't it too late?
Wasn't the amnesty or amnesia of my own decreeing and applicable not even
to one, to me, and in that case weren't we all excused
from class? And yet the board of governors certified me; I became a vicious citizen,
not even to blame for what ills dunces harbored
in God knows what unimaginable slums, for as long as I chose to occupy my seat
cooperating with the forces of eternal law and order yet unwilling
to compromise friends, neighbors, orderlies, the giraffe at the zoo,
who even now moves toward me on unbending legs,
though his designs are far from clear. From whatever is happy and not
unholy, lead: The plan of the porch is quite an obvious one, and you know
what sliding doors mean and wherefore gutters conduct rain
to the abject earth, and turn around and absorb the shock of hearing the truth
told, once more, on an unforgettable day in early June,
which shall be all we need ever know of hearing quarrels inside out and then
reversing them so the abstract argument is pure and just again, a joy to many.

How much luckier I am, though, than they, who can see where I'm stumbling to during
    the day
and can rein in at night, between hedges. It's like
dangling far above the city streets, a kind of peace if you don't spoil it
by losing patience. Sure enough, other fun began while I was gone, a kind of imaginative
recycling of the days I'd crumpled and tossed out, and then their
dated shenanigans came to

seem crisp and well-presented, focussed, cropped; none of the "careful draftsman" in me
   could
cavil at that. Besides it was nice just being outdoors with something to say. An excuse
like a birthmark arose and flowered, still swimming upward past
the layers of the different civilizations, to Sun Lake. I could trundle my shopping cart
   past
the wicket and still be there, off the hook. I don't mind being mesmerized even for
fairly long periods but this was like playing tic-tac-toe with an automated
stone saint; the mock-orange note in it was strong and I'd come, I
remembered, chiefly to see my own reflection. Now, where was I? Where'd I put that
ticket of readmission to the bathers, who by this time were streaming out
in twos and threes. "Show us how to open a book like that." We gave them coffee
when it didn't go fast enough. Things seemed to pick up after that, though I felt a twinge:

Was it going to do it for me, this time, and them? Might we be forced to split up,
and if so, which half of the ladder is left standing? You don't want to hear it. And still
the cloister extends, deeper and deeper into the dream of everyday life that was our
beginning, and where we still live, out in the open, under clouds stacked up in a holding
   pattern
like pictures in a nineteenth-century museum: Forgive us
our stitch of frivolity in the fabric of eternity if only so that others
can see how shabby the truth isn't and make their depositions accordingly, regulating
the paths over which we have no control now, speaking out of concentrated
politeness into an ear which wishes to hear, but once we have finished
what we had to say (and we have nothing to say) the moment and any afterthoughts are
   scooped up
as though by a steam shovel and deposited *over there*, not out of sight.
And the contentious are sometimes with us as a smooth pavane on glassy but profoundly
turbulent waters. How to keep it going
when all is trembling violently anyway, the air and all things in it? Shouldn't we
abandon them? But no these are

pointlessly fussy caveats sunk, so as to test one, in the great gray
fabric of the unwinding highway: Don't let its apparent dignity fool you, and besides
they're free, and can and do say whatever they want to you; that doesn't
mean you have to respond in kind, but it helps. Someone is working on it,
providing heat in summer and air conditioning in winter, and get-well
notes arrive in every post; the top
of the volcano has been successfully glued back on, and who is to say we aren't
invited? The invitation, after all, arrived too, that was your name
beautifully chiselled into it. And ideas like fire
struck too quickly from flint seem to matter; your house or my house,
this time?
       I really think it's my turn,
but the variations don't let you proceed along one footpath normally; there are
too many ways to go. I guess that's what I meant. Why I was worried,
all along, I mean, though I knew it was superfluous and that you'd love me for it
or for anything else as long as I could sort out the strands that brought us together
and dye them for identification purposes further on, but you
didn't have to remain that generalized. A few anomalies
are a help sometimes, confetti that gets lost in the cracks
of some conversation and then you have to take it back again to the beginning
and start all over again, but that's normal, it's no cause for alarm, there are
more people out there than before. If you can think constructively, cogently,
on a spring morning like this and really want to know the result in advance, and can
accept the inroads colorful difficulties can sometimes make as well as all the
fortunate happening, the unexpected pleasures and all that, then there's no reason not to
rejoice in the exterior outcome, sudden
mountain-face, the abrupt slide
into somewhere or other. It will all twist us
closer together, under heaven, and I guess that's what you came about. See these
polished stones? I want them and I want you to have them. It's time, now.
      [. . .]

So that's it, really. How all that fluff got wedged in with the diamonds in the star
    chamber
makes for compelling reading, as does the heading "Eyesores," though what comes
    under it,
e.g., "Nancy's pendant," is a decidedly mixed bag. The proper walk must be aborted
and tangled hope restored to its rightful place in the hierarchy of dutiful devotions
for it to matter at all to "the likes of" us, and get booted to the rear
of the compartment. We were talking about cats, I said you should have one
not so much for companionship as for the extreme urgency of not letting it out of the
    bag,
if you should be so lucky as to possess one of those too. You always thank me
for my suggestions even when I can see they haven't gone over too well, and this
was one of those times. We chatted some more about cats and other pets
and then parted on an amiable note, what I would call one. And all during the succeeding
weeks there was no word, nothing on the radio, what we call the wireless. You'd think a
    line
like "HUNT MISSING GIRL" might have turned up in the papers, but the actual
    situation
was otherwise. A standoff. A phantom so strange in its implications it defies
. . . classification. Otherwise, how his beans were cooked
made absolutely no difference to him. In fact he seemed to lose interest in his
    surroundings
daily. I remember including that in one of my reports. If he asked for a nail file
it would be to stab playfully at the pillow, or occasionally to clean his nails,
never to file them. Once I even saw him reading a detective novel upside down.
I was too upset to include *that* in my report, as you may imagine. And secretly he
wheedles favors out of us; the older nurses are more susceptible. If he wants to
wind up sidelined, in the dugout, that is OK with me, but I don't see why *I* should be
    expected
to sign the warrant for his release. I have other, more important, things to do, besides.
Getting that bit of lacquer repaired is just one of them, but you get my drift,
I fear, then too I've traditionally been the indulgent, mild-mannered one,

who thought nothing of taking an afternoon off to play golf if the weather was right
as it is so seldom in this inclement land. When I asked about the new monitors
someone brought in I wasn't expecting a sermon on the necessity of staking out one's
territory the very same day, but there it came, with a hurricane in its pocket for good
    measure.
And when no one was betting on horses, there were the nags to feed,
the grooms' quarters to be kept in proper order, liveries to be pressed—it all came
gushing down on me like a bushel of affectionate children. It is lucky I am
old enough to keep my head, faced with the demands on my time. Even a computer
would get riled sometimes. Now I am more interested in "easy living,"
though more than ever feeling a need to keep up appearances, impress the neighbors
with the latest electronic *trouvaille*. Yet I never let down my defenses
for a moment. I am what some people would call "hard," though
I'm really a pussycat underneath the austere façade. Speaking of cats, when was the last
time you spoke to one, calling it by its name? Out here on the prairie things are much
    too quiet
though we all know each other and share memories and stratagems
for coping with loneliness and disloyalty from time to time. In some ways
it's a life, or something you'd have no difficulty recognizing as such, but I wonder,
how are they going to fit me in at the end? Will my birdcage be draped
with some expensive Liberty fabric to suggest eternal peace, just as I was getting used
to the lively round of tea-parties and exhibits
some are over-attached to, but when you think
about it, what's wrong with a little pudding? Sprinkled with coconut, perhaps?
And then in the evening you get down to business, but you can't think clearer then.
Here there is no mist to admonish one, no pretzel sticks either,
and one knows very well what one wants to be
and can imagine a fancier existence anywhere. This has to get broken off here
for the reason things do get broken off: It's amusing. Love,
The Human Pool Table.

    [. . .]

Sometimes to stimulate interest in other titles we
try to encourage a different angle such as the Near East with its walled, secret gardens,
jacaranda petals that fall all day into the basin. And the hours,
peeled off one after the other like onion skin, yet there is always more:
some curve up ahead. In fact
we never see all there is to see
which is good for business too: keeps the public returning
these days of swiftly eroding brand loyalty, so you can say: I beat him up,
my competitor, and now I'm ready to do business with him again: Such
is the interesting climate we live in, all
shocks one minute, all smiles and surprises the next. I think I'll have the chicken salad
    oriental. I'll
wager you haven't one client in seven who can identify this, though the whole world
    knows of it,
this quite tiny key to success I hold in my hand. When the codger
returns I'll brusquely bring the question up again and you'll see. It's cooler
over here; the light forms a film at the windows
I first took for a curtain, a rash that won't wear off. Wait, now
he's ready to talk business. I have, sir, a handle on the truth
that could be of keen interest to you, a matter of considerable importance.
You can feel it when the lake is up and swans go flapping off
on various absurd errands, or when the phone rings and you hear his voice
before picking up the receiver, saying, It's me, I'm glad I waited
till you were in a different frame of mind, for truly this makes all the difference; no one
calls the woman who walks silently away, but later in the night
there are twists of tears and it seems as if someone shares your nervousness
about the awkward pauses that might ensue and has arrived at a plan of drastic action:
whisking the tablecloth off the laden table without disturbing a spoon is only part of it.
Giving up habits like compulsive hand-washing is another. Because you have no idea how
imperious their demands are; nothing can get closer to you as long as they are in the car-
    port

even though they too have nothing to say
and cannot justify their existence.

Other pleasures are folding the pillow and gazing mournfully into the face of the electric
    clock
when everything springs apart quite naturally and scrawled forms of people
are seen pacing the square in different directions; sometimes
one will hold on to another's head and then let go: It's my Sonata
of Experience, and I wrote it for you. Here's how it goes: The first theme is announced,
then fooled around with for a while and goes and sits over there. Soon the second
arrives, less appealing than the first or so it seems but after you get to know it you find
it deeper and somehow more human, like the plain face of an old lady who has seen
    much
but who has never been known to utter an opinion on anything that happens to her:
    quite
extraordinary, in fact. Then comes a hiatus in the manuscript:
The last bits of it keep seeming to move farther and farther away, like houses
on a beach one is leaving in a speeding motorboat: Wait, though!
isn't that them we're approaching now? Of course—we had been going around in a
    circle
all the time, and now we have arrived at the place of resolution. The stakes are high
now, but you couldn't tell it from the glum air of things: bored crows, seedlings.
And then, what passion
brought you to your knees? Suddenly your whole face is bathed in tears, though no one
saw you cry. This kind of makes me review my whole plan of action up to now; fishing
    around
for a handkerchief to hand someone does that to a person, I think, don't you?
And it will mean staying up later which in turn will screw up
tomorrow's well-laid plans, and then suddenly everything ends in a climax, or a cataract.
I think this *is* the way it was supposed to be, though I can't be sure now, so much has
    happened;

it will look better on a cassette, which is where I wanted it anyway, so I guess

we can go home now, each to his own bed, for each of us has one: That's what "calling it
   a night" means.

But I never meant to disturb anything, or harm a hair on your head; that would have been
   false

to our beginnings, and nothing could stand up to that, nothing good I mean.

As it builds, the power changes too, but in the

same direction it was carelessly aimed in long ago, before any of us got involved

with what we now consider our living, when it was free. And the strain grows, steadily,

though there are many scenes played for comic relief and the classic agendas are still

reenacted when people get together. Not quite late-twentieth-century panic, but sobering
   in its

simple difference which can scarcely be demonstrated. All the people we knew and the
   songs

we sang are on our side, sinking imperceptibly

along with us into Old Home Week. Except it's not. And we cannot see the bottom

of these issues; they have outgrown us; which made the eye in the church shine even
   brighter

when it finally opened. Meanwhile, over the scruffy skies of New York, a doubt hangs

like a jewel, a melancholy melon-color that could be the correct shade of mourning

in heaven, pitting all that we said against us. Why, it's right there in the *procès-verbal*,

only I don't feel too good. I just want to be absorbed in countries you were never

allowed to develop a taste for, yet I have no reason to go anywhere,

to be at your side, every place seems as mortally insipid

as every other place, and I've got used to living, like a toothache; I can stand

what's coming, but that doesn't mean I don't have to like it. Some mornings are quite
   pleasant:

A Florentine wonderment drips from the sky as putti with picnic baskets descend

to the enameled sward, and I don't have to ask you how near you think that lighthouse is,

or the blond warehouse: You find me in them. Is it asking too much

to want to be loved, just a little, and then to be satisfied with that? Of course not,
but the police are everywhere. You can't even order a drink without feeling one of them breathing
down your neck. And you apologize profusely, like the ridiculous twit you are.
Where is it written that men must go out in the afternoon without a hat?

In the real world things were going along about as well as could be expected, that is,
not quite satisfactorily. We were deceived in our reckoning,
but could still salvage some things like a decent emolument and self-respect. But in many ways
things were different now. Even the coastline had changed,
and the protective vacuum-packing around long-established major confrontations was no longer
mandatory. One sat at a kind of grillwork that used to be the kitchen table,
while outside hives exploded and buzzing insects darkened the air and we thought we knew
the year we graduated from high school, yet everything was suspended in an agitated trance.
Only, I knew where I wanted to go: to some mountains in the south covered with pine forests
and creeper. There, the silence causes you to will what you wanted to know without exactly knowing if it was OK.
                                    Here, curvaceous rocks brandish us; the squeals of
    "Put me *down!*"
are mere grace notes in this battle of stupid titans. Strangely, a few amenities do survive,
enough to seem to give the lie to so much stinking chaos which, since it hasn't overturned
everything, is therefore perhaps not what its pennant in the sky proclaims it to be:
walks by creeks, for instance. Yet by enabling all creatures to become something different,
not necessarily their opposite, the proposed bifurcating leads in time to impossible

extremities one could never apostrophize anticipating a benign outcome due to the
   dreamlike
imaginings at the center that produced them. Waves, like weather currents on the map,
drift and coagulate above us, like "the swan-winged horses of the skies,
with summer's music in their manes," absolving the map of all responsibility to present
   itself,
to be read as a guide, and offering in its stead only the inane fumes of incense
spiritual masturbation set alight, long ago, and this is the bread, the palaces of the
   present,
a time that cannot tend itself. Each year the summer dwindles noticeably, but the Reagan
administration insists we cannot go to heaven without drinking caustic soda on the floor
of Death Valley as long as others pay their rent and have somewhere to go without
   thinking,
behind the curtain of closing down all operations. It's all right, I
like doing the housework naked and can see nothing wrong with it,
nor do I feel ashamed of it. I'll be all right when the government goes away; its
police state may not recognize me, or, if it does, may just shrug. What can I want,
anyway? Besides cashing in my federal insurance policy, that is. But as usual life is a
   dream
of blackbirds slowly flying, of people who come to your door needing help or merely
wanting to attack you so they can go away and say contact was made and it's
your day in the barrel.
                              Those of us who did manage to keep control over our personal
   affairs
before it was all over are obviously not going to testify anyway. What would we have said?
That we confronted the monster eyeball to eyeball and blinked first but only
after a decent interval had elapsed and were then excused from completing the
   examination
before defenestration became an issue? I thought I knew all about you and everything
everybody could do to me but this hiatus is sui generis and I know not how to read it
like braille and must forever remain behind in my solicitations, derelict in my duties,
until a child explains it all to me. And then I'll weep

at mountainscapes, if it isn't too late. But say,
where are you going, and why do you walk that way? Oh, I'll be all right, provided
you shut up and don't read too much into the dog's picture. After all,
the mutt said he wanted it taken, and in the backyard, so how was I to know
there'd be hell to pay for even this seeming indulgence? And how did I get away
after fourteen years? I'm afraid that's one you'll have to save for the answer man, besides,
my time is up and nothing too terrible has happened, only clouds, wind, stone,
    sometimes
a distant engine, purring in the morning fog, before the others are up, but I can see it.
It unwinds shelteringly.
                But there were dreams to sell, ill didst thou buy:
not the man walking, the woman sitting on the toilet, the tuba-player unscrewing the
    mouthpiece
of his instrument and blowing into it, not the azaleas blooming in tubs; but the three
    policemen and the man
scratching his groin, turning to say something to someone you couldn't see; the women
who wandered up to you at a cookout, waiting for you to give them an affectionate
peck on the cheek; the marching band in Rio, and the one in New Orleans, who knew
the music very well, and played it as they walked; the African violets you called *violettes
du Cap*, white, pink and blue, doing nicely in a northern window: these, for your trouble,
you may have mastered and accomplished much else besides, not least turning yourself
    from a
slightly unruly child into a sophisticated and cultivated adult with a number of books
to his credit and many more projects in the works; as well as the unattractive dreamer,
stained with sleep, who grasps at these as they elude him, and grasps at still others
which elude him not, all the time swilling the taste of one in his mouth. Forgetful,
you hang up the receiver allowing others to get through: In your garden
there may have been much confusion but also attentive things growing, now cut adrift,
floundering for lack of direction from you. And we see it even in the tall houses
that fan out from here: Each has its family
who are not much concerned with you, but to whom a truce was offered, and who
    missed out on it

because of misplaced consideration for you; and then in the dark forests that slant down
ravines quite close to the town, whose emptiness you could have peopled
merely by taking them up, in conversation; and the vast, greenish-gray seas punctuated
with scudding whitecaps that are a mystery and will always remain so, but you could have
addressed yourself to that, at least, included them in some memorial address
at the proper time, and so saved a speck of righteousness for your otherwise unproductive
   antics, summoned
dazed spirits "out of hell's murky haze, heaven's blue hall," accommodated them even
as you sat beside me, reading or listening to music. Thus, it becomes time to relax
e'en so. Funny, isn't it? The last thing on your list, and now
it is being approached even as afternoon makes room for evening, when all our
aspirations shall be quietened. And if no post arrives, no hens cluck,
then it shall be just as if it had happened. Why? Because it's completed. Don't you
see the light, seeing the light? Now you see it, now you don't,
is about right, having given up all lust, all hope.
                                       There is a time for trying on new clothes.
Yet the spirits are still angry that you woke them, if that's what you did.
Dreaming a dream to prize—way to go, Thomas L. It matters not how puke-encrusted
the areaway, how charged with punishments the jazz-inflected scroll—this *is* your time,
   by golly,
so change your clothes and get it right. THIS IS AN ILLUSTRATION OF
   SOMETHING.
What people never really wanted to talk about—Stonehenge. Last year it was a phantom's
breath upset you. Incorporate it—no second chance will be given
but what an old man said, quietly sitting at a coffee table, eyes shielded from the light.
A blast of gramophone music veers into the shutters from time to time. In those days
   and
in that time you had to have a sister and brother and be known. Now anyone
may play, but the stakes, alas, are much higher. Few
can afford to lose. Yet you see brothers, and sons, caught in the lure of it,
swapping new clothes for food, in short doing all the things you were warned against,
like talking to strangers. I like that. I only wish more of 'em would listen to me, but they

too have their business to attend to, curious as it seems, even as your mouth waters
at the sight of one of them, who hurries on, unfeeling. It's at night they come back,
once they know they've got you, or can have you, and then the caterwauling begins
unchecked. How would you like a plastron front to wear with this? Of course you
   wouldn't,
but that don't keep none of them from trying to play the Ripper, more shitted against
than shitting, so then they *do* rise up, and it can be one hell of a sight,
especially for those unaccustomed to it. I prefer to sit here and "rest" my eyes.
Usually my hunches are good, but last week comes one of 'em, and they always
asks you for something, begs a little jam or some string, and once you give it
you're in their power. But you knew *that*. Then the fun begins in earnest, blows rain
down from all over, chopping-block sounds, you think mechanically of Mary Stuart and
   Lady
Jane Grey, holding on to your forelock, cap in hand, of course. I don't know how long
the mist and smog have overlain this city, the dreaded heat, rising out of the sewers,
that can seem like the odor of fresh-baked buttered rolls. Then you must go to it again
and fill out a new application, for they have mislaid the first.

We nightingales sing boldly from

our hearts, so listen to us:

First, a saxophone quartet told me we have lived too much
in the minds of others, have too much unguaranteed capital on deposit there.

Why are you here? Why did you scream?

Only that one told me a new-laid owl's egg is sovereign
against the gripes, and now I find you here too. I have found you out. You seem
convinced the killer is one of us. Why? Did a drowned virgin
tell you that, or Tim the ostler, or the one-eyed hay-baler

with a hook for a hand? Or was it something else—some letter
you might have received from some distant land
where all is peace under the umbrella-pines and a serpent guards
the golden apples still? Seal it didst thou,
to send it back across the water as a sigh
to those unknowable?
I'll be perfectly frank with you. Though the sun's crisply charred
entrails have slumped behind yonder peak, no one has stepped forward to claim
the amazing sum promised by the clerk. You know not one minnesinger has ever
reneged on a pledge. Until today, that is. When by the loose curtain's distracted
fall I spy the contour of an ankle, and the ferrous glint
of a meat cleaver. Go to the judge! Tell him what you have told me
and your daughter! Implore his mercy! Then if you dare
look round to see what impression your sudden fit of sincerity hath produced. I'll wager
    you
no one leaves the room, and that the tool chest be empty! Go on! Try it! Last one in's
a rotten apple, or a—a booby. That's my last offer. Chain me to the iron bedstead
and electrocute me, so help me, that's all you're going to get out of me, harden my
    arteries
to obsidian as they will, let the mostly empty bottles
be drained till not one drop remaineth in them. Now that the killer is caught
you can return the map to Mr. Isbark.

A little loathing,
a cautious wind that pads softly
like a cat about thine loin
and argues persuasively for a cease-fire, in which one might read
much if one were wide awake and made aware, in whose bright fire
hell's thistle gleams, a league or so away. Marry, save that alibi
for your autobiography. Serve me fresh drink, I'll drink on't.
They were getting closer to your name in the list; now,

nothing will remove that stain. So how's about a walk around the old neighborhood?
Eleanor's here too. You remember Eleanor. So, nice and easy,
until it becomes something like grub, or a slug, something shapeless and horrible
you can talk back to, even scream invective at—you've got the time. And meanwhile our
    balls and
asses got to shamble on. But the daddies were keen on it.
They all liked it. Yon dork in the petting zoo,
Who, what, is it?

Two nights ago when I was complaining about all the weather we've been having lately,
and about how no one can do anything about it—much as I'd like to—
I was still happy, but today it turns out the drought has been secretly installed for weeks:
We're only beginning to feel the brunt of it. Of course, measures will be taken

but that's scarcely the point. It won't like you any better for it.
And what about mud? If we lose it, we lose everything.
Distinctions would no longer get muddied. There'd be nothing in life to wriggle out of,
no ooze to drop back into. We need water, heaven knows, but mud—it's so all over the
    place,
like air, that the thought of its not being there is even scarier.
Like a home that must be abandoned quickly, whose carpets and wallpaper get that faintly
distressed look, earth would go on without us, leave us waiting in space
for a connection that never comes. Somehow we'd survive—we always do—but at what
    cost
of mud and cosmetics. Different forms of address
would have to be adopted. Manners would become pallid, and the plot of one's life
like a thin membrane in which one can still recognize the shapes
that brought us here, and lure us on, but stronger too, to survive business,
and that would wreck our average partygoing.

I live at the bottom of the sea now.
But I can still sense a stranger
even when far off
and count the threads of partings still to be formalized.

And later when we stayed talking quietly apart
in the roofless outdoor room, she had discovered
my beloved: "Well! *Improvvisatore!* It would seem God's wrath
has taken us both down a peg. I have my money. And you, I suppose, will wing it
as in the past of windy Marches and stifling Augusts we have known
together, nor regretted them once past, but say,
if not some thread, a token then, a coupon
for pats and fondlings? Was this thy gratitude for pats and fondlings,
to die like any other mortal ass?
And why, O dearest, could'st not keep thy legs,
that sacred pair, sacred to sacred me?" Why, then, risk it?
Why go after it? Anyhow, I left it in the crypt.

And all that time was much fussing, to-ing and fro-ing, and above all waiting
to see the result on the street next day. As it happened, it was a lady
in yellow, with nice legs, who turned to me and said: "Haven't you anything better to do?"
I wanted to cry back at her: "Yes! And these are those things! Let's
discuss your legs!" But I knew she couldn't imagine herself
filling more than the allotted space, one for her and one for herself,
so I said nothing, and she resumed her walking. *You*
understand it, though, don't you? I mean how objects, including people, can be one thing
and mean something else, and therefore these two are subtly disconnected? I don't see
    how
a bunch of attributes can go walking around with a coatrack labeled "person" loosely
    tied

to it with apron strings. That blows my mind. I see that you want to mean it, though.
Yes, I love it, but that doesn't mean . . .

A girl named Christine asked me why I have so much trouble at the office.
It's just that I don't enjoy taking orders from my inferiors, and besides,
there are so many other, nicer things to be doing! Sleeping while the navigator
is poised, adrift, and sucking each other's dicks is only one.
Travel is another. Dinard! Was ever such a place? And when you are tired
but not yet ready to return home, you can be that person again, the one who dragged you
here. And we made love on a car-seat
in the moonlight, except there wasn't much of it. And I was the only one!
These adventures had passed through my head while I was alone
and I thought I was having them. But you need an audience
for them to reach the third dimension. Spooks in the manor
won't do, no pre-school-age children. That night in the car, though . . .
Then we clambered down some rocks. There was a girl there who spoke of finance, of
    how
it's going to be the next most important thing. I said nothing, but wondered if I could
take my stories with me when that happens, maybe read them to others
who would appreciate them in the new financial age that offers better reception
to things of the future, like mine. False dewdrops starred her eyelashes,
and I realized we were no better off in this age than in any other, except
perhaps the Ice Age. How if we are always going to be doing things for each other
why then of course we'll miss the point, since what happens, happens off in a trailer
and we really know no more of each other than ever, and that is what
ought to be our tree, our piece of happening.
My *standing*, in the French sense of the word. How everybody accepts me
and knows they are going to see a nice sight. Forget it. None of it matters
except what I am as I am to others. Trees floating around. Hard-ons
and what to do about them. But it is arranged so that you cannot begin to play.
Knowing the rules doesn't help, in fact it's better if you don't. You have to

be *in* on it already. And if you aren't you can die very quickly, or spend the decades
shattered. Out of touch even with yourself.

How can I tell them that . . . or that *La Fille mal gardée* is my favorite piece of music?
I'm sorry. Look guys. In the interests of not disturbing my fragile ecological balance
I can tell you a story about something. The expression will be just right, for it will be
   adjusted
to the demands of the form, and the form itself shall be timeless though
hitherto unsuspected. It will take us down to about now,
though a few beautiful archaisms will be allowed to flutter in it—"complaint,"
for one. You will be amazed at how touched you will be because of it, yet
not tempted to find fault with the author for doing so superlative a job that it leaves
his willing but breathless readers on the sidelines, like people waiting for hours
beside a village street to see the cross-country bicycle riders come zipping through
in their yellow or silver liveries, and it's all over so fast you're not sure
you even saw it, and go home and eat a dish of plain vanilla ice cream. Noises that bit
   me,
would-be fanciers skulking around, after an autograph or a piece of your hair, no doubt.
And indeed there's no point in worrying about the author's tender feelings as he streaks
   along
and sees no shame in it, nor any point in your concern for his injured vanity, not that you
   don't
already love him enough, more than any writer deserves. He won't thank you for it.
But you won't mind that either, since his literature will have performed its duty
by setting you gently down in a new place and then speeding off before
you have a chance to thank it. We've got to find a new name for him. "Writer" seems
totally inadequate; yet it is writing, you read it before you knew it. And besides,
if it weren't, it wouldn't have done the unexpected and by doing so proved that it was
   quite
the thing to do, and if it happened all right for you, but wasn't the way you
thought it was going to be, why still
that is called fulfilling part of the bargain. And by doing so
he has erased your eternal debt to him. You are free. You can go now.

But the last word is always the author's so you might want to dwell a bit
more on the perfections of form adjusted to content, and vice versa too, by Jove! The
    gate
to the corral is open, and he's in there now, running around and around it
in a paroxysm of arrival that holds the attention of every last member of that little
    audience.

We're interested in the language, that you call breath,
if breath is what we are to become, and we think it is, the southpaw said. Throwing her
a bone sometimes, sometimes expressing, sometimes expressing something like mild
    concern, the way
has been so hollowed out by travelers it has become cavernous. It leads to death.
We know that, yet for a limited time only we wish to pluck the sunflower,
transport it from where it stood, proud, erect, under a bungalow-blue sky, grasping at the
    sun,
and bring it inside, as all others sink into the common mold. The day
had begun inauspiciously, yet improved as it went along, until at bed-
time it was seen that we had prospered, I and thee.
Our early frustrated attempts at communicating were in any event long since dead.
Yet I had prayed for some civility from the air before setting out, as indeed my ancestors
    had done
and it hadn't hurt them any. And I purposely refrained from consulting *me*,

the *culte du moi* being a dead thing, a shambles. That's what led to me.
Early in the morning, rushing to see what has changed during the night, one stops to
    catch one's breath.
The older the presence, we now see, the more it has turned into thee
with a candle at thy side. Were I to proceed as my ancestors had done
we all might be looking around now for a place to escape from death,
for he has grown older and wiser. But if it please God to let me live until my name-day

I shall place bangles at the forehead of her who becomes my poetry, showing her
teeth as she smiles, like sun-stabs through raindrops. Drawing with a finger in my bed,
she explains how it was all necessary, how it was good I didn't break down on my way
to the showers, and afterwards when many were dead
who were thought to be living, the sun
came out for just a little while, and patted the sunflower

on its grizzled head. It likes me the way I am, thought the sunflower.
Therefore we all ought to concentrate on being more "me,"
for just as nobody could get along without the sun, the sun
would tumble from the heavens if we were to look up, still self-absorbed, and not see
    death.
It doesn't matter which day of the week you decide to set out on your journey. The day
will be there. And once you are off and running, it will be there still. The breath
you decide to catch comes at the far end of that day's slope, when her
vision is not so clear anymore. You say goodbye to her anyway, for the way
gleams up ahead. You don't need the day to see it by. And though millions are already
    dead
what matters is that they didn't break up the fight before I was able to get to thee,
to warn thee what would be done
to thee if more than one were found occupying the same bed.

Which is how we came to spend the night in the famous bed
that James VI of Scotland had once slept in. On its head the imperial sunflower
was inscribed, amid a shower of shooting stars. I say "imperial," though by day
he was a king like any other, only a little more decent perhaps. And next morning the sun
came slashing through the crimson drapes, and I was like to have died. Although my
    death
would have encouraged a few, it did not happen then, or now, and still that me
as I like to call him saunters on, caring little for the others, the past a dead

letter as far as he's concerned. So that I wrote to her
asking if *she* cared anything about the way
he was going about it, and did she know what others had done
to stop him in similar circumstances. Her reply, brought to me late at night, when no breath
of wind stirred in the treetops outside, caught me unawares. "If to thee

he offers neither apology nor protest, then for him it is a good thing. For thee,
on the contrary, it augurs ill. If I were thee I'd stay in bed
from dawn to evening, waiting, at least until the sun
disappears from our heavens and goes to hector those cringing in the house of the dead.
There can be no luck in harvest-time, no tipping of the scales, while yet he draws
    breath."
I thanked her emissary and tiptoed out without telling him what I thought of her.
How extraordinary that as soon as one settles on a plan of action, whether it be day
or darkest midnight, someone will always try to discourage you, citing death
as a possible side-effect. Yet I could not, would not, dismiss my beloved boy. No way
would I proceed along the sea with no one to bounce my ideas off of but me.
And so we two rode together. It was almost late afternoon by the time we reached "The
    Sunflower,"
as the gigantic, decaying apartment complex was named. A noted architect had done

it right once, with open spaces, communal nurseries, walkways. Yet when he had done,
no one liked it. People refused to move in. It was cold and impersonal. To thee,
however, it seemed a paradise. The long, alienating corridors which the sun
sliced through at regular intervals were as confusing as a casbah; the dead
tennis-courts and watchtowers seemed a present sent by death
to distract you while you waited, always for her
touch. That said, there was plenty to do at night, while during the day-
long siesta one dreamed, and brooded not, and felt fairly good. No hog's breath

stirred the rusting weeds in the little yard in front of the veranda. Like me
you too chose to put a better construction on these things than perhaps the case
    warranted; at any rate, bed
always solves everything, at least for the time being. I went out and plucked a sunflower
but it was empty, the birds had eaten all the seeds. Surely there's a way

to avoid feeling lonesome *and* sorry for oneself, but up until today, no way
has opened before me, I'm *both* those things, though one would suffice. What's done
is done, they say, yet I can't help wondering whether, on a different day,
you might have turned around and walked back to where I was lying face down in bed
and told me all the love, all the respect you had for me, that was like a shining in you at
    me,
and we could have gone off to analyze our situation and add up the particulars. *Your*
    breath
was your own private property, of course, and you cared little for mine, but in the case
    of her
father being in the news and so many other officials who had turned out to be dead,
perhaps in a few years' time we would have forgotten all that, to live, sunflower
and sun, in periods of rain and drought, as they do in Africa, and never fear the sun.
It is written, and played on the African thumb-piano, that those who to thee
go, and return, unremembering, are earmarked for a lonely, unpleasant death,

and those to whom thou goest never grumble, even at the prospect of death.
Therefore it is urgent that we all, pursuers and pursued, be moving in the common way,
for that is the only way to outwit death, none-too-clever though he may be. To thee,
I say, stand, as though on a ladder picking apricots; your back should be to the sun,
and all will pass. You'll be satisfied, you'll see. No need to shake the sunflower
husk for dried kernels. Indeed, all the grasses are long dead;
the reaching angles of the thorn-tree branches barely jerk erratically in the breath
of the savannah. If I thought for one instant that the day

of the week spelled out protection for me, or that my own misdeed would trickle off me
like water from a duck's back, sure and I'd have done what any decent-minded preacher
   would have done:
I'd place bunches of fresh rue and meadowsweet in glass jars filled with water near the
   bed.
I'd point with my stick not at her sins but to the shy, closed flower of her womanhood,
   her

puckered glen of swansdown, and there would have been an end to it, unless her
parents had some say in the matter. We two have lasted almost until death,
and still nothing shields us from the aspirations of the sunflower;
even at night you can hear its ever-unquiet breath
that makes of life a station on some suburban railway.
Too bad you did what you did; I, meanwhile, was lying in bed
and caught the rumble of the vans of approaching day.
"This is my day, even though it belong as well to many who are dead.
I say it not in a spirit of possessiveness, only as a fact. Indeed, I pass it to thee
as generations of aspiring lovers and writers before me have done.
Look, this is what was done to me, written on me. Take it from me."
She stood up and began to do a little dance, then as abruptly stopped, noting the sun

had passed the zenith, and was waiting to be relieved by a replacement-sun.
In all our lives I still continue to try to make headway, and though to her
what I do never makes much sense, I do it anyway, for thee.
Scratching around one is sure to uncover bits of the ancient way;
meanwhile I am reasonably well-fed, clothed and happy and spend nights in a bed
that seems beautiful to me. We used to laugh; with every breath
we'd take, some new funny thing would point a moral and adorn the day,
until at last the earth lay baking in the heat, and the sunflower

had the last laugh. "Be strong, you that are now past your prime! When you are dead
we'll talk again and see how you understand this thing men call death,
that is in reality but a shadow of what God has done
to others, to the sun and to me."

I awoke, yet I dreamed still. It seemed that all had been destined for me
all along, and as I had traveled in fear, and alone, always the sun
traveled with me. At night one sleeps in fear of wetting the bed
but he makes amends for that by pointing to our eventual death
as a teacher would point with a wand to the solution of a problem on a blackboard. His
   way
is as inscrutable as a fox's. He brings to full bloom the cornflower and the sunflower,
then lets them slip into oblivion. Why? If I knew the answer, I wouldst tell thee,
but since thou sufferest much, I'll vouchsafe that the way of the dead
is as a lightness to our dreaming, a sense of gaiety, of irresponsibility. She in her
longing realizes much, and would tell it to us, but the breath
is gone. Still, there'll come a time and not too far off when all we have done
returns to charm us; we can go back, taste, repeat it any day.

So for the moment, although tomorrow is our day,
the sun shines through the meshes. You can have me
for anything I am, or want to be, and I'll replace you with me, introduce you to the sun.
When summer calls, and people wish they only had a way,
and nights are too thick, and days have barely begun to be spoiled, I'll riddle thee
about what we heard before we came here, how much is already done.
The moral of the story however is that the ubiquitous sunflower
knows the secret and cares. As a door on its hinges, so he in his bed
turns and turns, and in his turning unlocks the rusted padlock of death,
that flies apart and at once I am shriven. Take me in, teach me her

ways, but above all don't leave me for dead:
I live, though I draw only a little breath.

The story that she told me simmers in me still, though she is dead
these several months, lying as on a bed. The things we used to do, I to thee,
thou to me, matter still, but the sun points the way inexorably to death,
though it be but his, not our way. Funny the way the sun
can bring you around to her. And as you pause for breath,
remember it, now that it is done, and seeds flare in the sunflower.

And left it that way, and then it kind of got shelved. It was a missing increment,
but as long as no one realized it was missing, calm prevailed. When they did, it was well
on the way to being a back number of itself. So while people cared, and some even wept,
it was realized that this was a classic, even a generic, case, and soon
they called attention to other aspects of the affair. No one ever explained how a trained
competitor of long standing would just bar itself from the case that way, there being no
evidence of self-interest, except insofar as loving a sun constitutes one. They shied away
from this one, and it was with no love
or self-pity in its heart that it betook itself then down the few stone steps leading
to the crypt. Here, at least, peace of a sort reigned, better than the indifferent bog
of schnorrers and nay-sayers it had kept company with for so long, a whole season, and
    the unlovely
atmosphere that had soured that season at its close was not recognized here: It was a
    currency
no one had any use for. If this left one like sailcloth, with the grained and toned
texture of one who has seen much, and still wishes to help, why all the better: One could
    go
farther and fare worse than entertain the possibility of such a journey, a *voyage d'affaires*
that will consistently be fun at any given moment. And so, though stalks heavy with the
mothy, mopheaded bloom may tremble next August, that is a thing of the past; the sun

purges its mind of all negative thoughts, granting
equanimity with the largesse of one who has too much, and
causes people to re-examine their attitudes. Maybe get some rain?
Are sherbets more glorious now than formerly? So this small, piecemeal uncurling
    exposes
vast sheets of preoccupations that the sun's firmness can in many cases
cause to evaporate before their expiration date. A hound-shaped fragment of cloud rises
abruptly to the impressive center of the heavens only to fold itself
behind itself and fade into the distance even as it advances
bearing news of the channel coast. That is the archetypal kind of development
we're interested in here at the window girls move past continually. Something
must be happening beyond the point where they turn
and become mere fragments. But to find out what that is,
we should be forced to relinquish this vantage point, so
deeply fought for, hardly won.

from HOTEL LAUTRÉAMONT

(1992)

LIGHT TURNOUTS

Dear ghost, what shelter
in the noonday crowd? I'm going to write
an hour, then read
what someone else has written.

You've no mansion for this to happen in.
But your adventures are like safe houses,
your knowing where to stop an adventure
of another order, like seizing the weather.

We too are embroiled in this scene of happening,
and when we speak the same phrase together:
"We used to have one of those,"
it matters like a shot in the dark.

One of us stays behind.
One of us advances on the bridge
as on a carpet. Life—it's marvelous—
follows and falls behind.

AUTUMN TELEGRAM

Seen on a bench this morning: a man in a gray coat
and apple-green tie. He couldn't have been over fifty,
his mild eyes said, and yet there was something of the ruthlessness
of extreme old age about his bearing; I don't know what.
In the corner a policeman; next, sheaves of wheat
laid carefully like dolls on the denuded sward,
prompting me to wish of dreaming you again. After the station
we never made significant contact again. But it's all right,
isn't it, I mean the telling had to be it. There was such fire
in the way you put your finger against your nostril
as in some buried sagas erupts out at one sometimes: the power
that is under the earth, no I mean in it. And if all the
disappointed tourists hadn't got up and gone away, we would still
be in each other's reserve, aching, and that would be the same,
wouldn't it, as far as the illustrations and the index were concerned?

As it is I frequently get off before the stop that is mine
not out of modesty but a failure to keep the lines of communication
open within myself. And then, unexpectedly, I am shown a dog
and asked to summarize its position in a few short, angular adverbs
and tell them this is what they do, why we can't count
on anything unexpected. The waterfall is all around us,
we have been living in it, yet to find the hush material
is just what these daily exercises force on us. I mean
the scansions of tree to tree, of house to house, and how
almost every other one had something bright to add
to the morass of conversation: not much, just a raised eyebrow
or skirt. And we all take it in, even laughing in the right places,
which get to be few and far between. Still it is a way of saying,
a meaning that something has been done, a thing, and hearing always
comes afterward. And once you have heard, you know,
the margin can excuse you. We all go back to being attentive
then, and the right signals concur. It stops, and smarts.

NOTES FROM THE AIR

A yak is a prehistoric cabbage: of that, at least, we may be sure.
But tell us, sages of the solarium, why is that light
still hidden back there, among house-plants and rubber sponges?
For surely the blessed moment arrived at midday

and now in mid-afternoon, lamps are lit,
for it is late in the season. And as it struggles now
and is ground down into day, complaints
are voiced at the edges of darkness: Look, it says,

it has to be this way and no other. Time that one seizes
and takes along with one is running through the holes
like sand from a bag. And these sandy moments
accuse us, are just what our enemy ordered,

the surly one on his throne of impacted
gold. No matter if our tale be interesting
or not, whether children stop to listen and through the rent
veil of the air the immortal whistle is heard,

and screeches, songs not meant to be listened to.
It was some stranger's casual words, overheard in the wind-blown
street above the roar of the traffic and then swept
to the distant orbit where words hover: *alone,* it says,

but you slept. And now everything is being redeemed,
even the square of barren grass that adjoins your doorstep,
too near for you to see. But others, children and others, will
when the right time comes. Meanwhile we mingle, and not

    [. . .]

because we have to, because some host or hostess
has suggested it, beyond the limits of polite
conversation. And we, they too, were conscious of having
known it, written on the flyleaf of a book presented as a gift

at Christmas 1882. No more trivia, please, but music
in all the spheres leading up to where the master
wants to talk to you, place his mouth over yours,
withdraw that human fishhook from the crystalline flesh

where it was melting, give you back your clothes, penknife,
twine. And where shall we go when we leave? What tree is bigger
than night that surrounds us, is full of more things,
fewer paths for the eye and fingers of frost for the mind,

fruits halved for our despairing instruction, winds
to suck us up? If only the boiler hadn't exploded one
could summon them, icicles out of the rain, chairs enough
for everyone to be seated in time for the lesson to begin.

Come on, Ulrich, the great octagon
of the sky is passing over us.
Soon the world will have moved on.
Your love affair, what is it
but a tempest in a teapot?

But such storms exude strange
resonance: The power of the Almighty
reduced to its infinitesimal root
hangs like the chant of bees,
the milky drooping leaves of the birch
on a windless autumn day—

Call these phenomena or pinpoints,
remote as the glittering trash of heaven,
yet the monstrous frame remains,
filling up with regret, with straw,
or on another level with the quick grace
of the singing, falling snow.

You are good at persuading
them to sing with you.
Above you, horses graze forgetting
daylight inside the barn.

Creeper dangles against rock-face.
Pointed roofs bear witness.
The whole cast of characters is imaginary
now, but up ahead, in shadow, the past waits.

1.

Research has shown that ballads were produced by all of society
working as a team. They didn't just happen. There was no guesswork.
The people, then, knew what they wanted and how to get it.
We see the results in works as diverse as "Windsor Forest" and "The Wife of Usher's
    Well."

Working as a team, they didn't just happen. There was no guesswork.
The horns of elfland swing past, and in a few seconds
we see the results in works as diverse as "Windsor Forest" and "The Wife of Usher's
    Well,"
or, on a more modern note, in the finale of the Sibelius violin concerto.

The horns of elfland swing past, and in a few seconds
the world, as we know it, sinks into dementia, proving narrative passé,
or in the finale of the Sibelius violin concerto.
Not to worry, many hands are making work light again.

The world, as we know it, sinks into dementia, proving narrative passé.
In any case the ruling was long overdue.
Not to worry, many hands are making work light again,
so we stay indoors. The quest was only another adventure.

2.

In any case, the ruling was long overdue.
The people are beside themselves with rapture
so we stay indoors. The quest was only another adventure
and the solution problematic, at any rate far off in the future.

The people are beside themselves with rapture
yet no one thinks to question the source of so much collective euphoria,

and the solution: problematic, at any rate far off in the future.
The saxophone wails, the martini glass is drained.

Yet no one thinks to question the source of so much collective euphoria.
In troubled times one looked to the shaman or priest for comfort and counsel.
The saxophone wails, the martini glass is drained,
and night like black swansdown settles on the city.

In troubled times one looked to the shaman or priest for comfort and counsel.
Now, only the willing are fated to receive death as a reward,
and night like black swansdown settles on the city.
If we tried to leave, would being naked help us?

3.

Now, only the willing are fated to receive death as a reward.
Children twist hula-hoops, imagining a door to the outside.
If we tried to leave, would being naked help us?
And what of older, lighter concerns? What of the river?

Children twist hula-hoops, imagining a door to the outside,
when all we think of is how much we can carry with us.
And what of older, lighter concerns? What of the river?
All the behemoths have filed through the maze of time.

When all we think of is how much we can carry with us
small wonder that those at home sit, nervous, by the unlit grate.
All the behemoths have filed through the maze of time.
It remains for us to come to terms with *our* commonality.

Small wonder that those at home sit nervous by the unlit grate.
It was their choice, after all, that spurred us to feats of the imagination.

It remains for us to come to terms with our commonality
and in so doing deprive time of further hostages.

4.

It was their choice, after all, that spurred us to feats of the imagination.
Now, silently as one mounts a stair we emerge into the open
and in so doing deprive time of further hostages,
to end the standoff that history long ago began.

Now, silently as one mounts a stair we emerge into the open
but it is shrouded, veiled: We must have made some ghastly error.
To end the standoff that history long ago began
must we thrust ever onward, into perversity?

But it is shrouded, veiled: We must have made some ghastly error.
You mop your forehead with a rose, recommending its thorns.
Must we thrust ever onward, into perversity?
Only night knows for sure; the secret is safe with her.

You mop your forehead with a rose, recommending its thorns.
Research has shown that ballads were produced by all of society;
only night knows for sure. The secret is safe with her:
The people, then, knew what they wanted and how to get it.

Let's make a bureaucracy.
First, we can have long lists of old things,
and new things repackaged as old ones.
We can have turrets, a guiding wall.
Soon the whole country will come to look over it.

Let us, by all means, have things in night light:
partly visible. The rudeness that poetry often brings
after decades of silence will help. Many
will be called to account. This means that laundries
in their age-old way will go on foundering. Is it any help
that motorbikes whiz up, to ask for directions
or colored jewelry, so that one can go about one's visit
a tad less troubled than before, lightly composed?

No one knows what it's about anymore.
Even in the beginning one had grave misgivings
but the enthusiasm of departure swept them away
in the green molestation of spring.
We were given false information on which
our lives were built, a pier
extending far out into a swollen river.
Now, even these straws are gone.

Tonight the party will be better than ever.
So many mystery guests. And the rain that sifts
through sobbing trees, that excited skiff . . .
Others have come and gone and wrought no damage.
Others have caught, or caused, darkness, a long vent
in the original catastrophe no one has seen.
They have argued. Tonight will be different. Is it better for you?

THE PHANTOM AGENTS

We need more data re our example, earth—how it would behave in a
crisis, under pressure,
or simply on a day no one had staked out for unrest
to erupt. What season would fit its lifestyle
most naturally? Who would the observers, the control group be?

For this we must seek the answer in decrepit cinemas
whose balconies were walled off decades ago: on the screen
(where, in posh suburbia, a woman waits),
under the seats, in the fuzz and ancient vomit and gumwrappers;
or in the lobby, where yellowing lobby cards announce
the advent of next week's Republic serial: names
of a certain importance once, names that float
in the past, like a drift of gnats on a summer evening.

Who in the world despises our work
as much as we do? I was against campaigning again,
then my phone started ringing off the hook. I tell you . . .
But to come back to us, sanded down to the finer grain
and beyond—this is what books teach you, but also
what we must do. Make a name, somehow,
in the wall of clouds behind the credits, like a
twenty-one-vehicle pileup on a fog-enclosed highway.
This is what it means to be off and running, off
one's nut as well. But in a few more years,
with time off for good behavior . . .

FROM ESTUARIES, FROM CASINOS

It's almost two years now.
The theme was articulated, the brightness filled in.
And when we tell about it
no wave of recollection comes gushing back—
it's as though the war had never happened.
There's a smooth slightly concave space there instead:
not the ghost of a navel. There are pointless rounds to be made.

No one who saw you at work would ever believe that.
The memories you ground down, the smashed perfection:
Look, it's wilted, but the shape of a beautiful table remains.
There are other stories, too ambiguous even for our purposes,
but that's no matter. We'll use them and someday,
a name-day,
a great event will go unreported.

All that distance, you ask, to the sun?
Surely no one is going to remember to climb
where it insists, poking about
in an abstract of everyday phrases? People have better
things to do with their lives than count how many
bets have been lost, and we all know the birds were here once.
Here they totter and subside, even in surviving.

In history, the best bird catchers were brought before the king,
and he did something, though nobody knows when.
That was before you could have it all
by just turning on the tap, letting it run
in a fiery stream from house to garage—
and we sat back, content to let the letter of the thing notice us,
untroubled by the spirit, talking of the next gull to fly away
on the cement horizon, not quibbling, unspoken for.

[. . .]

We should all get back to the night that bore us
but since that is impossible a dream may be the only way:
Dreams of school, of travel, continue to teach and unteach us
as always the heart flies a little away,
perhaps accompanying, perhaps not. Perhaps a familiar spirit,
possibly a stranger, a small enemy whose boiling point
hasn't yet been reached, and in that time
will our desire be fleshed out, at any rate
made clearer as the time comes
to examine it and draw the rasping conclusions?

And though I feel like a fish out of water I
recognize the workmen who proceed before me,
nailing the thing down.
Who asks anything of me?
I am available, my heart pinned in a trance
to the notice board, the stone
inside me ready to speak, if that is all that can save us.

And I think one way or perhaps two; it doesn't matter
as long as one can slip by, and easily
into the questioning but not miasmal dark.
Look, here is a stance—
shall you cover it, cape it? I
don't care he said, going down all those stairs
makes a boy of you. And I had what I want
only now I don't want it, not having it, and yet it defers
to some, is meat and peace and a wooden footbridge
ringing the town, drawing all in after it. And explaining the way to go.

     [. . .]

After all this I think I
feel pretty euphoric. Bells chimed, the sky healed.
The great road unrolled its vast burden,
the climate came to the rescue—it always does—
and we were shaken as in a hat and distributed on the ground.
I wish I could tell the next thing. But in dreams I can't,
so will let this thing stand in for it, this me
I have become, this loving you either way.

AUTUMN ON THE THRUWAY

Say that my arm is hurting.
Say that there are too many buts in the sky today.
Say that we need each other off and on to see how it feels.

After which we'll promise to see to it, see that it
Doesn't happen this way again so that we may
Do something about it when it does happen.

Or that sincerity cover us with a cloak of shame
While our clothes are drying by the campfire this night
Of nights that means to go on and prepackage some of the original flame

In order to sell it so as to recoup some of the losses that
Started us on this path, repay the original investors.
How sweet then the bargain, the transaction. And you fear nothing

Notable, the skylight has been activated already.
Best to stay around admiring the new look on things.
Invent a new hat. Put on a growing season, staple the others

To the door hidden in the wilderness. And the losses be ours,
Not someone's in the sun, slut of some, weeping pointedly.
And the blinders—I have signed for them too.

Studies show it hanging in frost, in pajamas, up in the air
And a cerberus basks underneath, its own snowhole round
As an apple in belief. Water the tree in this area and it

Never expedites how much we were hoping to receive out of
What was promised originally, yes, traced on the tracing paper
Of some mood one day. We can never actually account for it

[. . .]

Or how lush its primitivism, in the beginning,
How steep the wall of its veil over face, or how
Far you had come, little

Spinner that that's all right now. How we come to be seen.
Yet we know we must pay

Not use up any money in between, for it

To become us, and then all lost, a second time
But in a time the merry neutral wisdom is gathered, to be sewed

Into the lining and you must cherish it there.
Never believe a false passport to the land of chocolate and bees'
Reasons and be forelost, freedom from a refuge
That took over once you began to get used to it. No, this other

Hand is the wish I bury and keep for you, really the only one
Beside me long, into a tense's dense conditions
And then you tear, tearing: O how long was it going to be for us

Until the scenery lay quiet like a beloved dog's head under the hand,

For what was moving to be moving, for it to have courted an aspirin
And lost face at the quarry edge. Hand me that theogony
And then get lost, don't read me my rights, please get out of here

Until I can think and then two more of us, for a day, come to where we two
Parted and it is on a day. I can't think
How it completes my thought but I never knew how that was going to begin.

    [. . .]

Nor did it mean anything for anyone growing up then.
We were merely—"sentimental" about describes it, yet that can too be loving
In one's breath, provided other people also move around in it,

Disturbing it. It's no Volga but it's vast and dreary and it moves,
Keeps on moving. And so it is a show window at Christmas,
Brimming with lights, with more suggested memories than it could deal with, and we,

Well we help it along for our sakes, which is to say not very much.
We thought about it so often. How many figures I had rehearsed
In the garret where you could see your breath, whomping

My sides from the cold. Now, to have written it, merely,
Seems tepid, a kind of clashing conundrums thing, and
People walk out in the middle of it, rustling programs, tears spatter

The hateful embroidered lace, O why not tear off that Juliet cap and throw it
With the papers of dubious cleanliness, anything so
As to avoid the recrimination of a look that says you did just what you did,

No other, and how is it now for you. Stupid spruces tremble at
Stucco corners and why is this not to be attributed to the hand
Of some vengeful but well-meaning deity too? Why are we alone

Held responsible for the way everything gets to look, why are we admonished
Every time we walk out and see things starting to be the way again
They probably were in the near past, just yesterdays ago, when we haven't changed,

Only coarsened, merely from staying around a few too many seconds, an expression
That hardens while the photographer tries to focus on it, that's enough
For today, this day at least. And how much farther he tries to follow when you

[. . .]

Have passed under the willows' swinging garlands, past the sweep
Of the stream where you sink in up to the ankles, on to the drought and out,
And he says, what a fine time, why how much to be here,

Only you don't come round. Please send somebody to finish
Or our nails may be chipped, our locusts blighted, our hoarfrost dispelled by a breath
That who wants to enjoy the risk of? Not him. Not me, certainly,

Though what you ask for is not infrequently what you get.
Under an upturned cartwheel hat she looked up, so solemnly silly
That for a moment you had to forget to outtake her. And her drink needed replenishing.

So in the long run all of it takes us far from the sea of what we were as individuals
And more from the time when all that mattered, mattered as to a single
Individual too old for the part, though a pair. How it's possible to see

How far apart we were on most issues, and the European cooks it differently,
Besides, and set against the plainness of American lives it melts like a wall and
Rivulets, runnels drain off it as though from a roof, rushing to join you

In the gutter, and where the growing begins askance
This time. No more frankness, it is apt to cloud, to
Give off steam in the time it takes to distinguish one accent from the truth.

So the lovely second theme is somewhat marred
By buried memories of revenge, and when the time comes to
Reinvent the initial phase, why, all but grinning stupidly, it hands

Its cards to another player and takes off in the direction of the pond.
Wait! But another's daring solution will never rescue twice the omen
That hankered for more polity, and beside us though we were of no mind

[. . .]

To reckon it into what we were being elaborated by. Myrtles fall,
Crape drapes. The spear
Is slowly lowered as for the last curtain.

You've got to decide what your name is going to be,
What to do about it. By what ring we are decoded. Tangles
Of snake-grass and more, though it wouldn't

Do to talk about it, would it? Why, since I have come home from school,
Why must I intend it? Who is the person who wants this? How many
Guests has he invited, where do they come from? Who isn't

In on the trail? Now his men have departed. They have been sent away. Does that
Mean they won't be back? Do we ever avoid our own reckoning, even
When the moist, mild sky smiles and the portcullis is up,

The drawbridge lowered, the road delighted to wind
Into a newly dapper landscape, pointedly new, and it runs away
With us, sweeps us up into something, some way to be

With pleasure and not be too long about it so the mood stays
But isn't fixed? If only I'd known what I was getting into
That day in Arizona, I'd have taken another detour, but you see

When you see gravel, you think roadbed, automatically, forgetting how little
It takes to set anybody off, buzzing into dreams. Old papers and
Memoirs. Feet under the desk. A tiny girl who smiles and is prepared.

What year was that? Who was in power then? By what
Sin have we been burned? And did the president point
His pointer at the blackboard to the word "articulate," and did

    [. . .]

Those feet reiterate the premise, damp down through the ages, fresh, yes,
But so ancient, like an ague. Teeth chattering, all proceeded to the dump.
After all, it would be time soon.

After all, nobody knows how to make this any more. You can't
Find us in their lounges. Soon, soon, however, the overpass takes us home.
The leaves are spent, lying in a ditch. Girls gone. The music, the horses took off.

THE LITTLE BLACK DRESS

All that we are trying most defiantly to unravel
is waiting, close to the path. Yes,
but the pace is both relaxed and insistent,
a swimming up from under. Your plan sounds fine.

I knew a brunette once in Omaha,
he said, and that struck us as news. He hadn't
been out of the truck long. On the dank ground the new
willow leaves lay, a reproof to him and us.
Why can't the clay bind us more firmly still,
until he can read,
get something out of these notations that arrive
every day, like letters, O not in the empty house.

They watch the blue snow.
It is the fifth act in someone else's life,
but here, on Midway Island, reefs and shoals interfere
with that notion. That nothing so compact
as the idea of a season is to be allowed
is the note, for today at least. It is Tuesday morning.
They sing a duet of farewell
to their little table, and to themselves as they were
When they sat at it. Noon intersects with fat birds
the rhythm of dishes in the cupboard. My love,
he seems to say, is this the way it is for you? Then we shall have to leave
these shabby surroundings for others, but first
I want to plant a kiss like a star
on your forehead. The ships are knocking together at the quayside,
the lanyards struck, there is more moving
than we were intended for, as we clear out
nodding to the caryatids we pass. Perhaps they will sing to us.

And in a summer house somewhere in Russia
a clematis soaks up the heat. One can think without breathing
of the blue snow that invades the fields, a curse some obscure ancestor
once let fall and now it's the custom, duly serenaded each season
before the apples rust
and the idea of winter takes over, to be followed in short order
by the real thing.
If all of us could lead lives of razoring things out of the newspaper,
filing them on pincushions . . . but no. There is the father
and morning to be dealt with, and after that the students arrive.
The rhythm is broken up among them.
That was a cold year, but not
the last. It will be remembered.

    [. . .]

Why is it you always ask me this, and this:
is there no question behind the arras of how we now meet
seconding each other's projects, our emotions? Or is that too weak
as a question, though strong enough as an affirmation, so that we again go out
from each other? One shades one's eyes automatically, though the sky
is dark. "We have no place to go" (the fifteenth
major situation), and if God decrees we like each other, someday
we will meet on a stone up there, and all will not be well,
but that is useful. Great rivers run into each other and graves
have split open, the tyranny of dust plays well, there is
so little to notice. Besides we have always known each other.

Except for that it was automatically the century
before this one. Thus we are made aware of the continuity
of times that were, and time itself is revealed
not as a series of rooms but a single corridor
stretching into the truth: an alpine pasture, with a few goats
and, in the distance, a hovel. It is high noon. Dinorah,
who has lost her goat, sings the mad scene for which her life
has been a preparation, sings it out of daylight, out of the outcropping
of rock overhead, out of the edelweiss and cowslips.
Now it is the turn of the mountain god
but he refuses to play. The blue snow returns. Shopfronts are boarded up.

Still one should never be in a hurry to end, to contrast the ending
with the articulations that have gone before. True, these are merely space,
but one in which lives can take on a single and sparing sharpness
that is an education in itself. This is one life
as we thought it over, and there are other songs, some too true to mention,
others of little weight, optional, cut from most editions
but waiting silently in place where they are expected.
The story falls, mountains conspire, brooks hesitate,
the storm endures.

IN ANOTHER TIME

Actually it was because you stopped,
but there was no need to,
the forest wasn't too dark, and yet,
you stopped and then went on a little way
as though to embarrass the idea of stopping.
By then the everything
was involved in night:
cars were discharging patrons in front of theaters
where light swelled, then contracted
into tiny slivers. Then listened.

A kind of powdered suburban poetry fits
the description, and isn't
precisely it. There was no briskness,
yet things got quickly done.
The cartoon era of my early life
became the printed sheaves and look:
What's printed on this thing?
Who knows what it's going to be?
Meanwhile it gasps like a fish on a line.

It is no doubt a slicker portrait
than you could have wished, yet all
the major aspects are present:
There you bent down under the waterfall
as though to read little signs
in the moss and it all came to life
but quietly. There is no way to transcribe it.

LE MENSONGE DE NINA PETROVNA

This slave brings me tea,
and happy, I sit for a moment, a spare
moment. Time under the tree passes,
and those things which I have left undone
find me out! O my spirit shall be
audited! and unknown readers
grasp the weight of my words
as their feathery hulls blow away
leaving the crabbed and sullen seed
behind. And how many of these shall grow?
Really I thought it was autonomous
as the birds' song, the vultures' sleep,
under crags to whom virtuous
dreams come and torture them awake:

All alone lest someone
approach too near, in a fever
that binds the edge of sleep
where it blurs to hysterical necessity,
in these hours I am someone.
A patch of damp cannot ever overcome
the hurricane that blows where it wishes,
and the Christmas tree ornaments may well be
dispersed, that look so perfect,
hanging together,
as must we all, to the distant cheering
of high-school students at a game
who mean no harm
but their kind words cannot save us
    [. . .]

or quite leave us alone
as one hand of the clock homes
in on its chosen numeral.
Costumes and memorized poems are the order
of this night
as through an enormous pastry tube
clouds ooze around the stars, lest
(so brittle and unimportant are they)
the wherewithal be lacking
to bring earth into some semblance
of unity under the sky
that mocks us and will never
let us be entirely
all that we were someday to be.

KOREAN SOAP OPERA

My sister and I don't seem to get along too well anymore.
She always has to have everything new in her house. Cherished ideals
don't suit her teal, rust and eggshell color scheme.
Of course, I was a buyer when she was still on the street
peddling the Communist youth weekly. I have a degree
in marketing. Her boyfriend thinks I'm old-fashioned.
Well, I guess I do have an old-fashioned mentality.

What kind of a mentality
causes men to commit suicide in their air-conditioned glass boxes?
It has been a life of adjustments. I adjusted to the postwar boom
though it broke up my family. Some took their honor to the mountains,
to live on wood and water. But the investment years
wrought havoc with the landscape. Everything is modular now, even the trees.

Under the dizzying parabolas of the railroad bridge, where the thud
of laundry mallets used to resound, the swiftly flowing
current is like green cream, like baize unfit for fulling.
So old are the ways,
for lunch one might select a large smelly radish.
In the streets, as always, there is a smell of frying fish
no one notices. The rain cannot make up its mind.
Other people like it other ways.

I need to interact with postal employees, civil servants, that sort of thing.
Just being asleep isn't enough.
I must cry out against injustice in whatever position
sleep overtakes me. Only then will I have understood what the world
and servants mean by self-abolishment, the key, it is said,
to success. To stand and contemplate the sea
is to comprehend part of the package. What we need, therefore,

is market gardens bringing a sense of time with them,
of this time, honed to razor-sharpness. Yet the whole
scheme is invisible to any shareholder, and so the feeling
lessens, the idea that a composite portrait
may not be so important after all takes over like the shoulder
of a mill-wheel, slogging patiently under water, then back
to the zenith, where the watchword presumably is.
In schools they teach things like plus and minus
but not in the gorge, not in boiling mud.
Area residents were jolted to find what in essence
was a large swamp, pythons and all, in their communal front yard.
To me, this is insensate. I cannot stand the wind at my back
making of me nothing, to be handed
over, in turn, to this
man, this man. For though he weathered patiently
the name, the one that occurs to all of us, he went out
and came in, not in the best interests of abundance;
not, it seems, being anything but about to fall.

Here's a paradox for you: If the men are segregated
then why are the women not?
If the rich can survive dust-storms thanks to their red-and-gold liveried
postilions, then you are playing with an alphabet here: Nothing
you invent can be a plenipotentiary,
turn itself inside-out, radiate
iron spokes at the mini-landscape, and so side with a population
of bears, who knows? Who knows how much there can be
of any one thing if another one stops existing? And the word you give to this
man, this man, is cold,
fossil fuel.

    [. . .]

One snorts in the laundry, another
is broken beside the bed. A third is suspended
in a baobab for all the sins
no one ever knew, for sins of omission are like pearls
next to the sin of not knowing, and being excused
for it. So it all comes round
to individual responsibility and awareness,
that circus of dusty dramas, denuded forests and car dealerships, a place
where anything can and does happen, and hours and hours go by.

A DRIFTWOOD ALTAR

I'll tell you what it was like:
If you could afford it, you could probably have had it,
no questions asked. If it ran well, hugged the road well,
cupped your body like a loose-fitting suit, there was only
the down payment; the rest is future memories.
Of all those who came near him at this stage, only
a few can describe him with any certainty: a drifter
was the consensus, polite with old people,
indifferent to children, extremely interested in young adults,
but so far, why remember him? And few did,
that much is certain. I caught up with him
on a back porch in Culver City, exchanged the requisite
nod, shirt biting into the neck. How is it with you and some
who have no meaning, to whom nothing pertains,
yet the emptiness is always with you,
crowding out sadness, a drum
to which the pagan is alerted, glances are exchanged,
and someone, whom later no one can recall, slips out the side door?

In the bathroom there was considerable embarrassment.
One had taken off without notice, and in the sludge
that washes up on the beach are papers to be signed,
seals to be affixed. O why in this case bother a stranger, there are
enough of us to oversee the caring, the docketing; there is even
warmth on these chilly evenings of late winter, a no-season, remembering
how hot and sharp it was only a few seasons ago
when they wore their coats such-and-such a length
and cars drove by, even as they do now in certain
precincts where the roads are washed and small, trivet-shaped flowers
appear a moment and are gone, to appease the musk-god, most certainly,
and people spill out of lobbies and their greetings thicken like silt
in the runoff from a glacier and it is the standard attitudes

that are struck, there is no cry, no escape from them?
O certainly one of you must have known all this,
had it plotted for him ahead of time and said nothing: Certainly
one of you runs down to the road with the news, or to get help, perhaps.

Then the idol winks and pirogues with their slanting
rows of oarsmen are seen departing backwards with undue haste.
It is time to think of spring and in pockets of not extreme despair
or under the threat of a ragged-looking but benevolent cloud, a thought
occurs: We weren't always like this, something seemed to intervene
about halfway here; at any rate a great deal of action
scrapes what we are doing into shape, for the time being. Though I am lost
I can see other points on the island, remains of picnics nearer
than one had thought, and closer still the one who comes
to resolve it all, provided you sign a document
absolving others from their eternal responsibility, swearing
that you like this light, these birds, this rattling credo
as familiar as a banging shutter, and above all, promising not
just to go about your business but to do the thing, see it drained, emptied,
a box in which four seasons will again fit
just as they did once before fire took the sky
and airplanes in their spotted plumage were seen to waver, and sink, drifting
on the wind's tune that gets in cracks here, the same
old bore, the thing already learned.

For it is indecent to last long:
One shot of you aghast in the mirror is quite enough; fog mounts
gnarled roots of the trees and one could still
stop it in time. There has to be no story, although it is
bedtime and the nursery animals strike expectant, sympathetic poses.
And then in a quiet but tense moment the crossed
identities are revealed, the rightful heir stands in the doorway.

True, it is only a picture, but someone framed and hung it;
it is apposite. And when too many moods coincide, when all windows
give on destruction, its curfew anchors us
in logic, not reprehensible anymore, not even exemplary,
though emblematic, as some other person talking in an old car would be.

THE YOUTH'S MAGIC HORN

The gray person disputes the other's clothes-horse stature
just send us some water maybe
herding him onto the escalator for a last roll
and bitter, bitter is its taste

We don't pay contributors
just send us some water maybe
We'll talk about the new flatness
and bitter, bitter is its taste

I'll probably be sleeping with you sometime between now and next week
just send us some water maybe
I haven't made a threat that the army hasn't carried out
and bitter, bitter is its taste

Meaningless an April day hungers for its model a drawstring
just send us some water maybe
Billboards empty of change rattle along beside
and bitter, bitter is its taste

Somewhere between here and the Pacific the time got screwed up
just send us some water maybe
but my spelling, as always, is excruciatingly correct
and bitter, bitter is its taste

and I welcome intrusions like the sun
just send us some water maybe
and all around us aquifers are depleted, the heat soars,
and bitter, bitter is its taste.
[. . .]

First in dreams I questioned the casing of the gears the enigma presented
You're a pain in the ass my beloved
The twa corbies belched and were gone, song veiled sky that day
I have to stop in one mile

The century twitched and spewed gnomes from its folds
You're a pain in the ass my beloved
The mule-gray pilgrim was seen departing
I have to stop in one mile

I never knew the name for this brand of contumely
You're a pain in the ass my beloved
Believe me I wanted to play the shores are still beautiful
I have to stop in one mile

Here shall we sup and infest sleep for the night
You're a pain in the ass my beloved
Morning will surprise us with winds like variable coins
I have to stop in one mile

You're the truth in my cup, violet in the edge of memory
You're a pain in the ass my beloved
Retrieve me at my dying moment so shall our hearts decay
I have to stop in one mile

Remember the stone that sits beside you—
You're a pain in the ass my beloved
Sometimes they come for you and forget
I have to stop in one mile

SEASONAL

What does the lengthening season mean,
the halo round a single note?
Blunt words projected on a screen
are what we mean, not what we wrote.

The halo round a single note
makes one look up. The careful blows
are what we mean, not what we wrote.
And what a lying writer knows

makes one look up. The careful blows
unclench a long-sought definition.
And what a lying writer knows
is pleasure, hallowed by attrition.

Unclench a long-sought definition:
What does the lengthening season mean?
Is pleasure hallowed by attrition
blunt words projected on a screen?

KAMARINSKAYA

And it was uniquely the weather, O *bombes-glacées* university!

Had they actually built something there?
It was whose turn to find out.
Tremendous lashings of cloud were pouring in, from over there, they said.
Mouths choked with news, though no news in particular,
blocked the corridor. Later aspects were discovered,
developed, and as always, they fanned out in twos and threes
or stood a little to one side to discuss whatever was being discussed.
The great moment paradigm had arrived for all of us.
Some of us reaped instant benefits. That very afternoon
we were five looking at the sea; the shore began its pitiless interrogation
and we were glad of the cleft that produced nothing and knowledge,
the freedom, to wait.   The dentist moon hovered by the wire: *Sure,*
look in thy heart and write. But don't throw foreign articles.
And after coming down from the plateau, the heights, we are amazed
at the power of the possibilities enfolded in each thing but above all how long
they have lasted—longer than consciousness itself. We can go on building
and the structure, the shed that joins ours, will always be there,
kind, undermining. And the strength to be indeterminate
overtakes one. There are always laws, and people to break them; that's not the point.
What is is the majestic lineage that is merely nerve endings of the air, plus spice.
It's not often we get to point to something this way,
saying:

"It must be daring or I would not have done it,
not consciously; in my sleep perhaps. And yet there are tables near mine,
close enough to overhear, and all he says is Daddy brought you,
we must make it up. Make up anything you like. Steal it
from a magazine, no one will know the difference. Use its resonance
and throw the rest away, down the steep ravine into the dump.
That way the menace is erased. And the waitress asked sweetly

if there was anything else I would be needing and I said Swell,
it's the unpinning, the unrolling of the linoleum so soon, and I
who had dwelt in realm of fancy it was I who was coming too.
There was approval all around me
and a costly lamp-base where the seconds melted and in a
gash too deep for sleep I had plotted it already, I was being told;
the light and the fences had said it. I was being rushed from leaves to tall grass
not knowing whether I had made it or whether the others had, sure only of
one piece of information in the instant harbor: the one true way
to make a book and get out alive. Surely,
the bourbon sours have stopped; now will be the declaration
of the rest of the stairway, and then we'll see.
And it's true then a locomotive may pass through like an elephant and no
one raise their eyes. The time is past, she said.
But even this wan swan song looks like news to me—
there are so many others out and getting—
and whatever happens will be red and gold like a fire engine.
Now *he* said that *she* said that he didn't know where they put it
and *she* said that *he* said that the law was over soon, that in the interim of the land
not one of us was going to cry, but many, besides we'd see
what a disaster looked like, with the moon back there and people's lack
of attention." Then he got right out and said so. Did it. But the sheriff
and his men were there. Did that mean—? But a woman read the riot act.
Now all was song, and cleaving

to the spar, that precious one, thing
that always turns up, radiant, one for the books, you must tell
them about this, really. Did that mean we had been let out?
Listen, the password is like downtown, no peace
prohibited, we can get where we want now
and can't get to but the steep ride
is safe. What do you want with me anymore? True.

ELEPHANT VISITORS

Sweet Young Thing: "Why are you all down in the mouth?"
Testy Gent: "We're all in the business of getting older,
or so it seems; we're moving on. The daytime approach
can fail you. Sit on this moment,
pause on this deck. What if the earth fell on *you*?
But the dirty salad of lies, etc., about assassination
is approaching. Something has not been found."

Here, try the gloom in *this* room.
I think you'll find it more comfortable
now that the assassins have gone away.
Or got away. Take a week and shut off the engines.
But we do have to manage to stay here in the mountains, or at least
hover, in place. There are things I still haven't told you.
What is the state flower of Nova Scotia?
On whom do we depend
when we twist downward tangled in the parachute
and the ground is coming to greet us too quickly?
That's when you could use a newspaper,
but try and find one in the prairie. I was muffled
by the elegance of it all
but now I'll take one step if only to save myself,
yes, and others. Doctors

never tell you why these four-footed quadrupeds are friends,
if only foul-weather ones. There's a lot in envelopes,
and in a hole behind the house,
but if we think we're better in this instance,
give them something they WANT. Tasseled trees.
Until which time we sign off—wait, the lotus
wants to say something: It's MADE IN JAPAN.

RETABLO

After it had jiggled down it came out OK.
Drugstores sold it. You to whom this awful mission has been
entrusted are barred, of course, from commenting
while it is held up in the courts
and none of your family or lawyers can, either,
which is unfortunate at a time
when such a lot depends on being supple and risky, the way
you always were, of course,
except that now it isn't quite enough, is it,
as was the case on certain days
gray and blustery, but otherwise quite undistinguished, quite
unmemorable. You had to choose.
Did I forget to mention that? It came with the package
and had to be peeled off and mailed back, but even that
foretaste of doom didn't rate a footnote, while other, less
notable and possibly less objectionable aspects dropped
out of the stone forehead, leaving it black,
something to be pitied, almost.

So much more came untied during the swinging
of the bell ropes and of course the maddening pandemonium of the bells
themselves—they get right inside your head—
that someone would invariably stop to ask, Hey what is this
redemption stuff anyway, all this talk about bonds and escrow—
wasn't it supposed to be on a more spiritual shelf
where presences of sages nod and fall on each other,
falling asleep all over each other,
and at noon the terriers run and die as though these
treehouses were meant for someone else who would fit them out
differently, all spare and nautical? Captain, you've got to tell me,
what is this insane voyage about? I haven't even bought a ticket
and besides am on dry land heading back to see my aunts and cousin, aw,

have a heart will you? And these garbage-flecked
shoals beyond the barrier reef, you can't tell me those orange-
haired floozies are sirens! Hell, I can hear 'em.
And *I'm* going nowhere, that's for damn sure, as I know you
know in this vacuum you label interest in other people's lives,
in seeing how they accomplish what they set out to do.

Probably the rain never got loose
for all you know, but it did, it was like cellophane noodles escaping
from a slashed envelope. I had a transparent raincoat to prove it,
but it wasn't enough, that wasn't enough, nothing was enough to be quiet
in the little schoolhouse, but it *was* enough to know the last
class was over many seasons ago. There was something learned once but
it had drained out through a ring of rust in the middle of the floor,
and besides the desk-captains never kept such good time
any more, but of course there was less to know in those days:
only a few harness-bells, and a heap of dust and straw.
Which reminds me: Why are you shivering under that horse-blanket
when there's so much to be done by way of filing
the last perennials, each in its separate slipcase, and of not letting Jack get away.

He's got more to do; there's more to be done
than any of us ever dreamed of, whole pockets and mountains
of it, let into the side of a cloud hill.
Then the worrying starts, a fresh leak of pain
squirts through the tape and soon the bandage is loosened,
useless in the grass where I was standing all along, a picture
to myself. So the long rain waves drain;
there's a sense of compactness, or even nothing, though all the ships
have returned from Iceland, with stars, and with the scarves that sent them there.

QUARTET

Always

because I saw the most beautiful
name go down ahead of mine

I'm banished to an asteroid
perfect meld of soppy common sense
with somewhere a loose connection

only don't make me think it
always
I'm figuring out what went just before
with that which comes too late:

invitation to a pool party
where the hors d'oeuvres are free
as well as the first drink but not
the later ones
this was pretty late in the season

for me I told a tired invisible guest
but one must invade new premises
scout new locations
from time to time I said he seemed
to agree

that my date hadn't been seen in some time
oh well I was trying to lose her suppose
we go upstairs and just have a look round
flashbulbs popping
I said
well anyway as it is baked so shall it endure

[. . .]

and the coordinated midriffs be here
at 10:30 sharp no one moves
before every hand is on stage I
think I know what that meant he said
there'd be no more coffee and doughnuts
before this smooth introduction I believe I'm
one of your friends of course he said make room for Miss Scott

I suppose it's idle of me to worry
how other people will take the cold
it belongs to each of us like a blanket
and like fear doesn't go away
though it does go away in the evening
and return in the morning
and each of us deals with it
like bowels or bladder like

it or not I said we is each
a machine for milling or sorting whatever
gets digested or eliminated there's no
planning to stop for a while
taking a brief vacation
taking in some theater or old film
it's useless because bad
we pronounced ourselves part of the
joint agreement

and indeed I just meant to come back for a moment
to make sure I hadn't left anything behind
and lo and behold I am the central protagonist
in this cabana and all that was
going to be hid from me is hid
and everything looks quite normal

and so I shall approve the document
there's no earthly reason not to
is there
I said and he said no it's all past in the weather

and no matter what private associations are
set in motion by this train of thought no
change can ever be the result
I saw where he was leading
and it was centuries before I could disentangle
my sense of what I thought was right from the legal
obligation to bind everything into a sheaf
to recognize myself on your mirror
when we both returned to the dark pond
agreeing it best to nourish the affection
with toasts and witty consolation

rather than undertake a new epic
that might get bogged down in production
anything rather than those covered wagons
converging on a new day and he said I'm with you
I can't understand what the cue cards
mean about it snowing outside the sanitarium
solarium and is it true I am to spend my entire life meddling
with someone else's desires and then piecing
everything together just before it all blows up and I can
say yes once I had the meaning of it it was pretty good
and now all can see the meaning in it and I have forgotten
it all but it all still seems pretty good I guess he said

[untitled]

And now I cannot remember how I would have had it. It is not a conduit (confluence?) but a place. The place, of movement and an order: The place of old order. But the tail end of the movement is new. Driving us to say what we are thinking. It is so much like a beach after all, where you stand and think of going no further. And it is good when you get to no further. It is like a reason that picks you up and places you where you always wanted to be. This far. It is fair to be crossing, to have crossed. Then there is no promise in the other. Here it is. Steel and air, a mottled presence, small panacea and lucky for us. And then it got very cool.

[This poem was commissioned by the artist Siah Armajani for use in his Irene Hixon Whitney Bridge, built in 1988 in Minneapolis, Minnesota, on commission from the Walker Arts Center. The words of the poem are affixed to the upper lintels of the span and run in each direction across the bridge.]

JUST WEDNESDAY

So it likes light and likes
to be teased about it—please
don't take me literally. That winter light
should be upon us soon in all its splendor—
I can see it now—and the likes of the haves
shall mingle with the have-nots, to some point
this time, we all hope, and the pride encoded
in the selection process that made us what we are,
that made our great religions fit us,
will be deployed, a map-like fan so you can
actually sit down

and find us where we came from. True, some
at first claimed they recognized it and later
admitted they didn't, as though the slow rise
of history were just some tune. That didn't prevent others
from really finishing the job, and in the process
turning up points of gold that are we say these
things we shall have, now. And the jolly
carpentered tune merely played along with all that
as an obbligato, but on a day
took up residence in its own strength.
A weary sense of triumph ensued but it was the reality
of creation. There were no two ways.

And so one emerged scalded with the apprehension of this,
that this was what it was like. You gave me a penny, I
gave you two copies of the same word that were to fit
you like rubber ears. Is it my fault if in the dust
of the sensation something got knowingly underscored, defaced,
a shame to all the nation?
After all, it suited when you set out dressed

in plum and Mama was to meet us at the midpoint
of the journey but she got taken away and an old
dressmaker's dummy draped in soiled lace was substituted
for the intricate knowledge at this juncture.
The grass grew looser but closer together,
the flowers husky and fierce as trees. On the spiffy
ground no wagers were taken and a few minutes'
absence is the bee's knees. It behooves

you to depart if the moon is cowled.
That homeless blanket you gave up—
you should have sent them both years ago. A few
cronies still gather there where the shore
was explained and now the waves
explain it with renewed mastery and suds. Almost
time for the watchman to tell it to the lamplighter
and I'll be switched, after all these years.

Pardon my appearance. I am old now,
though someday I shall be young again. Not, it's true, in the near future.
Yet one cherishes a hope
of being young before today's children are young grandparents,
before the gypsy camp of today has picked up and moved
into the invisible night, that sees,
and sees on and on like a ritual conscience
that bathes us, from whose dense curves we know
we shall never escape. We like it here as the trial begins,
the warming trend, more air, even the malicious smile in the prefecture garden—
would we like it as much *there*? No, for we only like what we already
know, what is familiar. Anything different
is to be our ruin, as who stands
on pillars and pediments of the city,
judging us mournfully, from whose cresting gaze is no
turning away, only peering back into the blackness of the pit of water of night.

Once I tried to wriggle free of the loose skein of people's suggestions
chirping my name. One can do that if one is rich. But for others a bad
supposition comes of it, there is more death and pain at the end,
so that one is better off out of the house, sleeping in the open
where chiggers infest the lilacs, and a sullen toad sits,
steeped in self-contemplation. By glory I had
better know before too long what the verdict is. As I said I was changing
to more comfortable clothing when the alarm bell sounded.
Which is why I am you, why we too
never quite seem to escape each other's shadow.
Perhaps drinking has something to do with it
and the colored disc of a beach umbrella, put up long ago against the sun.

Yet even where things go wrong there is more
drumming, more clatter than seems normal. There is a remnant of energy
no one can account for, and though I try

to despise my own ways along with others, I can't help placing
things in the proper light. I am to exult
in the stacks of cloud banks, each silently yearning
for the upper ether and curving its back, and in the way all things
seem to have of shaping up before the deaf man comes.
O in a way it is spiritual to be out from under these
dead packages of the air that only inhibit
further learning and borders, as though these too came to see the sea
and having done so, returned
to selfish buildings enclosed by walls. Their conceit
was never again to be quite as apt as that time that is remembered
but no more, on a quilted sea of pylons and terminal anxiety
far from the rich robe, imagined and unimagined, as far as the pole
is from us. As around the pond, several rods away, the liquid
performance starts and repeats, endlessly.
We live now in *that* dust
but no one shakes it, no finish is yet prized, prized and forgotten.

As when we bumble, maintaining steadfastly that there is no life in the truth of us,
no bearings in the grass, and who cares anyway, why the salt
on his fingertip is life enough for us under the present circumstances,
something always focuses attention on all we have done since school,
how we were naked, and fell, and those
coming up behind dutifully picked us up and presented us as evidence
and the court in a major shift decided to hear the arguments
and all was sadness, it was decreed, for a while,
till pregnant pauses were abandoned, and miniskirts returned, and with them
a longing for a future of fashionable choices,
dotted earthworks in the comforting desert,
various fruits to assuage thirst
and the almost maniacal voice of your leader
reminding us of practical solutions so out of date they were all but forgotten.

   [. . .]

Far from fear of crowds stumbling,
what ought to incite you is a new hunger for all the angles of whatever
day this is, placed against the sandstone of undoubted
approval from many different quarters.
True, all that we hurled
returns to visit, and true too that the bayoneted
clock recovers, that composure is a gift
that sometimes the gods bestow, and sometimes not; their reasons in the one
as in the other case remaining inscrutable even to apple-
scented mornings where the light seems newly washed, the gnarled trees in the prime
of youth, and the little house more sensible than ever before
as a boat passes, acquiescing to
the open, the shore, the listless waves that distract us
out of prurience and melancholy, every time. Yet something waits.
I can hear the toad crooning. It's almost time for intermission.
The guest register awaits signing. It's another, someone's, voyage.

NO GOOD AT NAMES

We've been out here long enough.
The past recedes like an exaggeratedly long shadow
into what is prescient, and new—
what I originally came to do research on.
I have my notes, thank you. The train is waiting
in the little enclosed yard. My only duty
now is to thank all those who put up with me
and trusted me so long. It must have seemed
like a long process. My thanks are due, too,
to others with whom I never came in contact,
who may not have been alive, but
somehow we were in apposition, and as my pen
strikes out on its own, it is chiefly those others
I wish to remember. In a word, *merci*.

And at random stages of the journey he sees
what we were meant to see: underwear on a clothesline,
flying leaves, patches of dirty snow. It's true no one
ever tests you on these things, that nothing would have been different
if you hadn't seen them all, yet by emerging
they have become part of the picture, so vast and energetic
it gets seen by nobody. Later, in the station,
you greet a small group of close and not-so-close friends,
sparring about would the bargain have been different
if it had happened in something resembling a time-frame,
or a landscape, even a landscape one has only heard about.
And you show each other your clothes, smiling shyly,
and talk about the after-effects of the medication
everyone's taking these days, and it seems to have made
a difference, brought out the leaves in the public squares.

    [. . .]

Great travel writing has to be manufactured this way
for the desert's glitter to sink back into something tractable
and frozen antennae to balk at the day's closing prices.
A moment of horrible witchcraft isn't too much to be swallowed
for the land to become whole, and people wise
in the way that suits them.

IN VAIN, THEREFORE

the jetsam sighs,
flooding the front hall,
with the fragile violence etched
on the captain's forehead:

Some got off at the next-to-last stop;
others, less fortunate
were lost on the trail,
pines and mist carrying over
until the exit wicket

displaced all thoughts of a former, human time.
We, it was reasoned,
led lewd lives, belong with the bears.

A very few carry enough energy to
create a kinetic bonding arrangement.
These are the so-called sad ones
eating alone in restaurants,
drying their hair . . .

The dandelions are dead and the mud
of summer. They
tell of roasted meats, be oblivion
but a decade away
and the waterfall, unused,
is ruined, it is ruined, is not to stand.

A HOLE IN YOUR SOCK

A man walks at a city
as though veering off somewhere.
They extend arms, touch hands.
This is how it is done, every day.

My phone is tapped.
I wish to call the police.
Not, not obviously, part of the
"proceedings,"
the message takes control smoothly.

We contemplate the shells of crustaceans
long dead, waiting for the Bronze Age to end.
We go farther, fare worse.
And they gave us our little raincoat back.

Then the government gets into the act
and the others crowd in and out.
That was something, sainthood
of a sort. You have to take it.

They simply . . . die. And that's it.
When we come back
in fortuitous weather
the charm has multiplied beyond the sky,

is ever so contemporary,
as an ingredient should be.
The class marshals, boring thespians
have walked on. A teardrop
stands in the middle air.

This future does us good.

HOW TO CONTINUE

Oh there once was a woman
and she kept a shop
selling trinkets to tourists
not far from a dock
who came to see what life could be
far back on the island.

And it was always a party there
always different but very nice
New friends to give you advice
or fall in love with you which is nice
and each grew so perfectly from the other
it was a marvel of poetry
and irony

And in this unsafe quarter
much was scary and dirty
but no one seemed to mind
very much
the parties went on from house to house
There were friends and lovers galore
all around the store
There was moonshine in winter
and starshine in summer
and everybody was happy to have discovered
what they discovered

And then one day the ship sailed away
There were no more dreamers just sleepers
in heavy attitudes on the dock
moving as if they knew how
among the trinkets and the souvenirs
the random shops of modern furniture

and a gale came and said
it is time to take all of you away
from the tops of the trees to the little houses
on little paths so startled

And when it became time to go
they none of them would leave without the other
for they said we are all one here
and if one of us goes the other will not go
and the wind whispered it to the stars
the people all got up to go
and looked back on love

TOKEN RESISTANCE

As one turns to one in a dream
smiling like a bell that has just
stopped tolling, holds out a book,
and speaks: "All the vulgarity

of time, from the Stone Age
to our present, with its noodle parlors
and token resistance, is as a life
to the life that is given you. Wear it,"

so must one descend from checkered heights
that are our friends, needlessly
rehearsing what we will say
as a common light bathes us,

a common fiction reverberates as we pass
to the celebration. Originally
we weren't going to leave home. But made bold
somehow by the rain we put our best foot forward.

Now it's years after that. It
isn't possible to be young anymore.
Yet the tree treats me like a brute friend;
my own shoes have scarred the walk I've taken.

THE MANDRILL ON THE TURNPIKE

It's an art, knowing who to put with what,
and then, while expectations drool, make off with the lodestar,
wrapped in a calico handkerchief, in your back pocket. All right,
who's got it? Don't look at *me,* I'm
waiting for my date, she's already fifteen minutes late.
Listen, wiseguy—but the next instant, traffic drowns us
like a field of hay.
                    Now it's no longer so important
about getting home, finishing the job—
see, the lodestar had a kind of impact
for you, but only if you knew about it. Otherwise,
not to worry, the clock strikes ten, the evening's off and running.

Then, while every thing and body are getting sorted out,
the—well, *you* know, what I call the subjunctive creeps back in,
sits up, begs for a vision,
or a cookie. Meanwhile where's the bird?
Probably laying eggs or performing some other natural function. Why,
am I my brother's keeper, my brother the spy?

You and Mrs. Molesworth know more than you're letting on.
"I came here from Clapham,
searching for a whitewashed cottage in which things were dear to me
many a summer. We had our first innocent
conversation here, Jack. Just don't lie to me—
I hate it when people lie to me. They
can do anything else to me, really. Well, anything
within reason, of course."

Why it was let for a song, and that seasons ago.

ABOUT TO MOVE

And the bellybuttons all danced around
and the ironing board ambled back to the starting gate
and meaningless violence flew helplessly overhead
which was too much for the stair
Better to get in bed they cry
since Zeus the evil one has fixed his beady eye on us
and will never come to help us

But out of that a red song grew
in waves overwhelming field and orchard
Do not go back it said for if there is one less of you
at the time of counting it will go bad with you
and even so, many hairy bodies got up and left

Now if there was one thing that could save the situation
it was the cow on its little swatch of land
I give my milk so that others will not dry up
it said and gladly offer my services to the forces of peace and niceness
but what really does grow under that tree

By now it had all become a question of saving face
Many at the party thought so
that these were just indifferent conditions
that had existed before in the past from time to time
so nobody got to find out about the king of hearts
said the woman glancing off her shovel The snow continued
to descend in rows this rubble that is like life infested with death
only do not go there the time should not be anymore

I have read many prophetic books and I can tell you
now to listen and endure
    [. . .]

And first the goat arose and circled halfway around the ilex tree
and after that
several gazed from their windows
to observe the chaos harvesting itself
laying itself in neat rows before the circled wagons
and it was then that many left the painted cities
saying we can remember those colors it is enough
and we can go back tragically but what would be the point
and the laconic ones disappeared first
and the others backtracked and soon all was well enough

Today I would leave it just as it is.
The pocket comb—"dirty as a comb," the French say,
yet not so dirty, surely not in the spiritual sense
some intuit; the razor, lying at an angle
to the erect toothbrush, like an alligator stalking
a *bayadère*: the singular effect of all things
being themselves, that is, stark mad

with no apologies to the world or the ether,
and then the crumbling realization that a halt
has been called. That the stair treads
conspired in it. That the boiling oil
hunched above the rim of its vessel, and just sat there.
That there were no apologies to be made, ever
again, no alibis for the articles returned to the store,
just a standoff, placid, eternal. And one can admire
again the coatings of things, without prejudice
or innuendo, and the kernels can be discreetly
disposed of—well, spat out. Such

objects as my endurance picks out
like a searchlight have gone the extra mile
too, like schoolchildren, and are seated now
in attentive rows, waiting trimly for these words to flood
distraught corners of silences. We collected
them after all for their unique
indifference to each other and to the circus
that houses us all, and for their collectibility—
that, and their tendency to fall apart.

THE LOVE SCENES

After ten years, my lamp
expired. At first I thought
there wasn't going to be any more this.
In the convenience store of spring

I met someone who knew someone I loved
by the dairy case. All ribbons parted
on a veil of musicks, wherein
unwitting orangutans gambled for socks,

and the tasseled enemy was routed.
Up in one corner a plaid puff of smoke
warned mere pleasures away. We
were getting on famously—like

"houses on fire," I believe the expression
is. At midterm I received permission
to go down to the city. There,
in shambles and not much else, my love

waited. It was all too blissful not
to take in, a grand purgatorial
romance of kittens in a basket.
And with that we are asked to be pure,

to wash our hands of stones and seashells—
my poster plastered everywhere.
When two people meet, the folds can fall
where they may. Leaves say it's OK.

WELL, YES, ACTUALLY

To whom it may concern: Listen up.
About a year and a half ago a young man was in my office.
This young man,
whose name was Michael,
was the friend of another young man I already knew, Frederick by name.
Well, the upshot of it was, Michael,
who had pulled himself up by his bootstraps, wanted
to know the secret of things already not so secret,
like: Water, does it seem swollen, or how much does it weigh
when all the water molecules have been withdrawn,
and to whom does one address oneself after the correct answers have been passed
    around?
I told him, as best I could,
indeed, as I have told others in the past, that such soft
mechanisms, such software, can't be regulated, and if it could,
no one would want any answers. Well, he just sits there,
dumb. Then, as the call of the crow renews itself
across valleys and pastures, in the island at night,
the answer speaks in him too. Only it can't, he realizes right away,
ever be repeated. Or someone would pull nettles in exasperation,
slapping them all over the place, and then what devil-may-care
attitudes it pleases you to ration out will be flat as paper,
flatter than shadows peeled off of pavement. But I digress.

In this town, near this tree, a school rose proud and tall
once, and from a distance many were seen going in and out of it
as the bell sounded the hour from its red, hacienda-like tower.
And sure, mutts wandered in and out too,
and radish sellers. Well, one
man, a rustler to all appearances, wasn't happy
with the school and all its appurtenances: desks, faucets,
blackboard erasers and such. He thought it was a pity

that some come to learn and enjoy, while others plait
their tresses idly, in cool shadow, and read no book
and add no sum, the while the milk sours
happily, in the shade. And children from out of town would come
and look down at the others, and they too would fall to quarreling
until the teacher summons all, and says,
"Blessed children, my children. I would have it no other way
but this." And the man thinks, if that's what they teach you in school,
maybe I should go back to school. For I'm a loner, I warrant,
and loners never learn, though they may know the one thing
nobody else knows, or, by the same token, needs.
And a shadow fell across the fields
of radishes: This was the real, the genuine article,
and all other speculation had been slightly but sadly displaced.

And they thought about it. The teacher thinks about it to this day,
wondering where she went wrong,
why the prisms no longer irradiate electric colors
and the Bunsen burners cause no retorts to fume
and gurgle over, over the long desks that were.
These are the apples of my crying,
she says, the ones they never brought me, and I,
I am too distressed to dream.
Well, don't you think Michael and Frederick heard about it
and were the first to offer their condolences? But first
they swept all the chalk bits into a neat pile
and dedicated it to the stranger, and to the teacher they offered
the product of Pomona's blissful yearnings,
who dances alone all day by the sea, inebriated,
yet loves us as only a modern spirit can.
And they propped the door open
with a wedge-shaped piece of wood, so that it stayed open all the time.

MYRTLE

How funny your name would be
if you could follow it back to where
the first person thought of saying it,
naming himself that, or maybe
some other persons thought of it
and named that person. It would
be like following a river to its source,
which would be impossible. Rivers have no source.
They just automatically appear at a place
where they get wider, and soon a real
river comes along, with fish and debris,
regal as you please, and someone
has already given it a name: St. Benno
(saints are popular for this purpose) or, or
some other name, the name of his
long-lost girlfriend, who comes
at long last to impersonate that river,
on a stage, her voice clanking
like its bed, her clothing of sand
and pasted paper, a piece of real technology,
while all along she is thinking, I can
do what I want to do. But I want to stay here.

MUTT AND JEFF

But what he does, the river,
Nobody knows.
—HÖLDERLIN, *"The Ister"*

Actually the intent of
the polish remained well after
the soup was nailed down. Remnants to cherish:
the sunset tie old Mrs. Lessing gave me,
a fragment of someone's snowball.

And you see, things work for me,
kind of, though there's always more to be done.
But man has known that ever since the days
of the Nile. We get exported
and must scrabble around for a while
in some dusty square, until
a poster fragment reveals the intended clue.
We must leave at once for Wabash.

And sure enough, by the train side the blue-
uniformed bicycle messenger kept up easily
and handed me the parcel.
"Ere the days of his pilgrimage vanish,"
I must reflect on exactly what it was he did:
How lithe his arm was, and how he faded
in a coppice the moment the yarn was done.

Still, the goldfish bowl remains
after all these years like an image
reflected on water. It was not a bad thing
to have done what I have done,
though I can imagine better ones, but still
it amounted to more than anyone ever thought

it would. The mouse eyes me admiringly
from behind his chair; the one or two cats
pass gravely over or under my leg from time to time.
The point is there's no bitterness,
not here, nor behind the scenes.

My sudden fruiting into the war
is like a dream now, a dream palace
written for children and others, ogres.
She was braining my boss.
The day bounced green off its boards.
There's nothing to return, really:
Gumballs rattled in the dispenser, I saw
my chance for a siesta and took it
as bluebottles kept a respectful distance.

COVENTRY

There was one who was put out of his house
and another that played by a pond
of a lateness growing,

one that scalded his hand.

And now, he said, please deny there was ever a house.
But there was one and you were my mirror in it.
These lines almost convey the comfort of it,
how all things fitted together in their way.
But it was funny and we left it—
her address, her red dress.

Just stay out in the country a lot.
You have no house. The trees stand tentless,
the marmoreal floors sweating . . .
A delusion too.

Good thing. Good luck.
You'd have to stay in Coventry.
But I'm already there, I protested.
Besides, doesn't any leaf or train want me
for what I'll have stopped doing when I'm there,
truly there? Yet who am I to keep anything,
any person waiting? So we diverged
as we approached the city.

My way was along straight boulevards
that became avenues, with barrels of trash burning
at each corner. The sky was dark but the blue light in it
kept my courage up, until the watch spring
broke. Someone had wound it too tight, you see.

Then I could only giggle at the odd bricks,
corners of tenements, buildings to be leased.
I fainted, honey.

And I never saw you again
except once walking fast
across the Victorian station
lit by holiday flares
yet strangely dumb and rumorless
like all the sleep and games that jammed us here.

AND THE STARS WERE SHINING

I.

It was the solstice, and it was jumping on you like a friendly dog.
The stars were still out in the field,
and the child prostitutes plied their trade,
the only happy ones, having learned how unhappiness sticks
and will not risk being traded in for a song or a balloon.
Christmas decorations were getting crumpled in offices
by staffers slumped at their video terminals,
and dismay articulated otherness in orphan asylums
where the coffee percolates eternally, and God is not light
but God, as mysterious to Himself as we are to Him.

Say that on some other day garlands disbanded
in the fresh feel of some sea air,
that curious gulls coasted from great distances
to make sure nothing was getting more than its share
of pebbles, and the leaky faucet suddenly stopped dripping:
It was day, after all. One of those things like a length of sleep
like a woman's stocking, that you lay flat
and it becomes a unit of your life and—this is where it
gets complicated—of so many others' lives as well
that there is no point in trying to make out, even less read,
the superimposed scripts in which the changes of the decades
were rung, endlessly, like invading kelp, and
whatever it takes to be a simp is likely not what saved you
in time to get here, changing buses twice, and after,
when they sent you to your corner to lick
your wounds you found you liked licking
so much you added it to your repertory of insane gestures,
confident that sleep would punish those outside
even as it rescued you from the puzzle of the dance,
some old fire, thought extinguished, that now

blazes in the stove, and in an instant we realize we are free
to go and return indefinitely. Is that

what you meant by lasting? Oh, sure,
hedgerows are in it too, and the doves there and insects
and treed raccoons that eye one with frank disapproval:
"You unmitigated disaster, you!" I was pleased to discover
one could flatten or otherwise compress it, its Tom
Tiddler's ground having induced only a subcoma, a place
where grown men drink screwdrivers and giggle at the melee
that would certainly have resulted if someone, some prince regent or sheriff,
hadn't been in charge, while the long day moped
and opened the fan of its grievances, harassment
being the only one that stands out in the blur now, after such distance.

The steed returned home alone, requiting all previous loves.

   II.
To have been robbed of a downturn
today, I have drunk some water,
rollicked in the texture of a late,
unfinished sonata,
sinking into snow,
falling forward in the oratory,
violent as the wolf's cue and anything
you take from that side of the ledger
only beware of boredom, boredom-as-spell.

Then, slipping into the gentle jacket of
my having to know why everybody passes me,
how I cursed that heir, braided that subway

of signals seen only from behind,
the old rug and its mug—all were madness for me,
yet only dust. And as I undid its much-stitched
frogs, a near melancholy approached
from across the lake—little slivers
of sense unbent, that were right about it all
in their way, though I unlatched these tears,
bleached for the occasion.
                                    The stairs knew
it was under them, but by the same token couldn't acknowledge
the enormous debt lifted from the mountain's brow.

And the same foreman, the same teacups jingle still,
following a localized pattern,
uncovering what till now has been everyone's pill.

   III.
The nude thing was taken around
to various ambassadorial residences.

And on the day he had come home
to see her, her in the maze of
sandwiches some artisan proposed,
he was like a bee in summer.

Remember the reflexive mode, the soul
can live with that, or live behind
it he said, to no avail. The last
breasts caught up.
            [. . .]

And in morning like sugar she gave her head
to the toll-places the mind suggests.

IV.

words like so many tiny wheels
—JOUBERT

divide the answer among them
on the facade of the spinning jenny as it
approaches improbably,
a toxic avenger . . .

Later amid the hay of reasons
we sort out a sparse claim.
Was it to be thirty he dressed her
in black-and-white checkers of gingham,

or,

perforce, did the lad go athirst
thinking no doubt too late of the spincs,
pelage of mingled hairs and spines,
when all would have meant protection
for him from the main highway, the chief.

A porch

rattles in the near, clear distance.
There was never any insistence on a name,
though we all have one. Funny, isn't it?

Yours is Guy. I like "Guy," "Fanny" too,
and they grow up and have problems same as us—
kind of puts us out into the middle of the golf course
of the universe, where not too much ever happens,

except growing up, hook by hook,
year after tethered year.
And in the basement, that book,
just another thing to fear.

   V.
The problem
would have to have had so many other things wrong with it
to remain remonstrably a problem that we would have had to float,
it to its bottle of capers, I to my mound of gin,
for the others to see us and pretend not to notice.

That would have been the bonanza, the great volcano,
but as they say in Cheyenne, "Ain't some weekends no
more than sister days of the week when it comes to volleyball
and dimity shrouds," and aquarelles are for the masses
to live off of, when food and conversation run out.
I know because I was a kid with a banana,
but that's for eternity only. All other gaps open out
in the mind of the possessed. I'll be glad to

repeat what I said in court, but send
no lawyers after me, no *papier bleu*, if you please . . .
And the spider shinnied down the thread it was making as it did so,
curious about what other alarming event could be occupying this same moment,

and when he got there, well, it was too late. Death
makes no excuses and, by the same token, exacts none.
The race
is to the fit, and it's a great day for the race,
the human race, yes, but also the tent race,
and my husband is as a cored apple to me:
beautiful, sometimes, and in and out of the dark.

We cared less for each other
than any two people on earth, but the point is we cared.
Don't tell the scotties we didn't.
They wouldn't believe you anyway—it's just
that my mind is full of eyes, days like this.

    VI.
A silly place to have landed,
I think, but we are here.
The door to the dressing room is ajar.
A tremendous fight is going on in there.
Later, they'll ask and you'll say you heard nothing
out of the ordinary, now, not that day.
Madame had gone out . . .

So bring the scenery with you.
Midwife to gargoyles, as if all or something
were appropriate, you circle the time inside you,
plant an asterisk next to a kiss,
and it was going to be okay again, and the love
of which much was made settles closer, is a paw
against a wrist. Hasn't finished yet,

      [. . .]

though the bread-and-butter machine continues to churn out
faxes, each grisette has something different
about her forehead, is as a poinsettia
in the breeze of Rockefeller Center. I don't like
a glacier telling me to hurry up, the ride down is precipitous.
Then a smile broke out on the ocean face:
We had arrived in time for the late lunch.
The dogs were instructed not to devour us.
And so much that in the past
was kept in flavors of ice-cream sodas now jumps
into one's path. We'll have to
take note of that for tonight's return trip,
though silver sleighbells pamper us,
hint that we'll get to see the Snow Queen
after all, at long last, obscuring the fact
that somebody *was* running along the courtyard.
Then the janitor wasn't screwy, the mickey
he was to have been slipped was stuck in heavy traffic,
and all those conversations about carbon dioxide
were a smokescreen too. How brittle it all was,
in the way abstractions have, and yet how
much it mattered for those children: It was their
funeral, and they should have had a say in its undoing
by the lighthouse's repeated lunges.
He claimed it was to read Sir Walter Scott by.

No one ever questions *him*. That asparagus-like mien
wasn't made to encourage dolts and stutterers.
Yet I think a clue is back here
behind the sofa, where lost bunnies whimper
and press together. He *had* been a seafarer,
who knew where his last hamburger

had come from, and whose cursive signature adorned
the polished bullet. In a little while peace
would establish itself, welcome foreigners and venture capital,
and tides rush in to destroy
what little progress in unleashing the sense of things
I and my classmates had made. We were still
at the beginning of the alphabet, chanting things like "Tomes
will open to disgorge intuiting of our altered dates,
we stepchildren, who had no place to go, and nowhere
to be late, and brash breezes
play with our buoys. Still, a little consideration
might have helped, at that point." And time will be as precise
as a small table with a cordless telephone on it, next to a television.

VII.

Rummaging through some old poems
for ideas—surely I must have had some
once? Some people have an idea a day,
others millions, still others are condemned
to spend their life inside an idea, like a
bubble chamber. And these are probably
the suspicious ones. Anyway, in poems
are no ideas. No ideas in things, either—
her name is Wichita.

Later with candles coming to the
celebration, it occurred to me how
all this helps—if it wasn't here
we'd be like lifeguards looking for prey.
Look, one of them stops me. "Your
candle, sir?" Dammit, I know there was something

I was supposed to remember, and now I'm lost.
"Oh no you're not, the smile on that big
bird's beak should be enough to let you in
on the secret, and more." He's here to help,
the whole darn nation is, even as
tidal waves suck at its precipices and high-speed
dust storms dement its populace. One
will say he's seen an anchor in the sky—
why am I telling you this? It's just that the light,
violet, impacted, made a difference
for a moment
back there.

The bug-black German
heels and back areas, the long tilted
cloaks for sale, the others—yes,
they're still here?
Something must be done about it
before it does it itself. You know
what that will be like. The white tables with their
roses are so beautiful. It doesn't matter if the corn is faded.

    VIII.
I've never really done this before.
See, I couldn't do it. Does this
make a difference to you, my soul's
windshield wiper? See, I can try again.

Now, try to expose it.
We'll look back and it won't seem
so long ago. This late in Dec.

you go from day to night in 32 minutes,
the peonies ajar—

That which I polished
as a child stands up to me.
A peashooter blows away
the soldiers.

I have seldom encountered more libidinousness
on the road to the tracks. My shanty
looks okay to me now, I can live with it
if not in it,
who had the prescience—the prescience of mind
to buy a part of New York
while it was still a logo on someone's umbrella,
a rococo convict from the Laocoön tableau.
Those snakes get worse each season
the deaf man said
and he had reason
on his side, they were strangling his kid
and goat even as we talked in the parched
weather that was obscurely damp and white.
Next swamp we'll do better,
tidy up things, the davenport
that got thrown out, the kerosene lamp
you wanted for your henhouse. The stoves,
so many of them. The refrigerator:
Eskimos really do need them
to keep their food from freezing
you said to the teacher, and my eye
is dry, all the riddles come undone.

     [. . .]

Hot, swift choices
over the lake in May.
The old gray mare.
Violets blossomed loudly
like a swear word in an empty tank.
The fish mostly had gone home
the admiral repeated falling into
his habitual stammer—whenever he came
to the words "iron blow" it happened for him,
poor rich man, who despised the stall tickets
once he recovered from the rage
of being within us again.

And whether it was smoke on a balcony
or idle laurels that seem to creep
out of his books in the library
we were chastened—"by the experience"
and so went to bed and never read again.
It was glorious standing up in the various rain
to keep clear of the teeth but that changed nothing
fast like a fast game of checkers.
The kind of cry that can't be heard

yet others outside might know of
soon as the mist was sucked
up through a tube and the platonic curve
returned for various dignitaries to perch on
like members of the Foreign Legion or the French Academy.
Androgynous truths never shattered anyone's
complacency on Broadway even though they use thermal down
now (I thought it had been outlawed)—
beckoning though maybe not at you

as you come to evaluate
all the leaning together.

And the store models are free
for the asking—aye, that's just it,
"for the asking." What isn't? And who
can make that chirp
sound round in the eye of the traveling salesman—
taller than might have been expected, than Mont Blanc—
who sees the talisman perishing amid lichees
while others gape and walk back toward
Washington Square.

If I had night I would feed it to you
but I have something much better—the desire to run
away for president, with you
in my back seat. And whether butter
brings a smell of gas with it or the Beefeaters
look bloated, all is of some concern to us—
we didn't need to be separated before you knit that
sweater as a plenary indulgence: shimmering
with only pastel colors like a life lived
near sunlight exclusively, like a page turner's
romance with the page and the soloist.

It breaks into thunder:
thought that comes to you,
a safe haven from the shipping.
Lo, a low hill welcomes those who wish
to climb its flanks, to its summit
just over the near horizon, blue and cream,
the colors of my navy she said, I'll bet yours

are similar too. That was why I had to play
my gray cape, the lost card

no one is ever conscious of having.
And if we had something for the stew,
some salt or something, why that could go in too
as long as land could still be sighted
to the left, a silver crow's nest in which all
lost objects, blue Christmas tree ornaments, arise
and sing the national anthem of Hungary
and the river garments come together with a clap
to shield those who never previously wore them
and the gold tooth extracted from a brooch
join in the general clamor
of do-gooders—the common sort of folk
all over us like a coat of burrs.

Once the bear knew he headed back to his cave.

Winter wasn't clear yet
but all the days of the year were tumbling out of its crevices,
the chic ones and the special-interest ones,
and those with no name upon them.
Everything looked slight
which was all right.

Then the magician entered his chamber.
Too bad there are no more willows
but we'll satisfy his bent commands anyway,
have a party in the dark,
throw love away, go neck in the park,

fill out each form in sextuplicate—then let the storm
be not far behind, the old graves and swords
of winter erupt out of turn. It won't be bad
for us. You see, the penguins have stayed away too long,
ditto the flamingos. I think I can make it all
come together, but for that
there must be a modicum of silence.
Your ear's just the place for it.

IX.

New technology approaches the bridge.
The weir, ah the weir, combing the falls,
like the beautiful white hair of a princess.

In the oxidation tank he thinks
of fish, how strange they can get the oxygen
they need from the water, and then when it goes blank—
why, pouf! And you realized the past suffered
from housemaid's knee, and that when the present
came along, why no one would speak up,
and it just moved in, with pets . . .
For the medium future I had thought striped stockings
and a kind of beard like a haze, seen only
on certain ancient sun deities who walked
absorbed in fields, as children groused
and crocuses sputtered the unbelievable word.

Right, it's definitely our situation.
We can come out of it but not simply leave it.
It will die of having so many things in it,

like a barrel choked with leaves. Yet sooner or later,
you know, one is dipped in it
and spotted lawns, greatcoats emerge.
The cistern really was built
by the workmen while you were away.
It's alive and containing.
And so many horticulturalists sway,
inebriated with the hardiness
of the ranunculus, the gladiolus.
Even so, he asked us to leave him
alone, at night, wanted to think
or something, about love or something,
something that turned him on.

Only later when we came to bask
in his friendship, did that marine eye astonish us:
Out over so much plains, such doo-wop wind,
you'd think it wouldn't spell "ceremonial" to him.
But he merely shaved the numbers off, dawn removed
the fingerprints, and why I am with you
and these several elves, no one can piece together:
not Great-aunt Josephine or her mortician boyfriend,
not the robbers of the "School of Night" drawing.
And we shifted, you and I, causing the rowboat to take on water.
Strange, how a few decibels can make your day.

    X.
Of course some of us were more risible—then.
Stopping by an apartmentful of freeloaders
on a snowy evening, I was asked about the *other*

mysteries, and, forced to prevaricate, noted
that time was setting in.

As one gets peeled away from life
and distant waterspouts put their kibosh on the horizon,
just one message makes it through the triple filters:
Go easy. Your chums on this shore have
worked long and hard on the inclined-plane thing;
if you haven't any suggestions (and you haven't),
let them continue to think it was sorcery
that was lacking. The fact that no directional
arrows pointed the way to the mother lode
proves their greenery to them, and they begin
to reason: "The kitchen's not such a bad place,
if it's sinks you're after. Sure, Caruso was singing
somewhere behind the padlocked velvet door,
but if we stay—no, linger—here, the problem
will reverse itself. Tom and Jerrys all around."

As for the ritual endowment
so prized by the Coca-Cola girl, that only arrived later
to prove its wetness and wildness nonfatal
just before the sun came out and caked it.

We sure live in a bizarre and furious
galaxy, but now it's up to us to make it
into an environment for maps to sidle up to,
as trustingly as leeches. Heck, put *us*
on the map, while you're at it.
That way we can smoke a cigarette, and stay and sway,
shooting the breeze with night and her swift promontories.

XI.

But in the soul of man there are innumerable infinities.
—THOMAS TRAHERNE

There is still another thing I have to do.
I've never *been able to do this*
and I have this announcement to make
over all the streets, all the years we have been difficult
leading to this. This icon. That walks and jabbers
fortuitously or not. Bells splinter the ice
and I am away, on a trip somewhere. Kansas.
It doesn't matter for me
and matters so old for you, sobs distant as tractors.
We are the people we came to see
or might as well be, bringing cabbages as gifts,
talking nonstop, barbed wire stringing the trees,
cigar smoke bellowing.

It was all the same to us,
we came in and out,
were thoughtful as strawberries, and the great athlete overturned us,
made us obsolete, Now that was a day I can trace
with a little mental calisthenics
and find I know what I was doing, to whom
I spoke, the kings, carriages, it was all there.
And my knowing derives no comfort
from that parallel shelving of events.
No kind of nexus. As if the doll herself knew
what you weren't supposed to know, and survived the fall
from the attic window to incriminate you,

just before the draft swept her into the furnace.
The burning is beginning again.

But there are a giant two of us,
the remnant, or product, or a complex
bristling-up-around, then a feigning of disinterest
in a corner of the room, and the fuse ignites
the furniture with blue. It's earth-shattering, they say,
as long as you contain it,
and you have to, can. The brain-alarm is being recalled
but the message exists even with no words to inflict it,
no stanzas to be cherished. For we end
as we are forgiven, with chords the bird promised
caught in our throats, O sweetest song,
color of berries, that I lied for and extended
improbably a little distance from the given grave.

    XII.
A late glimmer read into it
what is not to be intuited,
only pressed, like a hand or pants,
as the sea presses against rock
for lack of anything better
to do—surrounded by buddies
taking a breather, it was always thus with you,
you who come close enough to me:
Oh, you've often found
clues in the garden where the hornets
and the robins make their nests;
clues on the stairway, in the vestry

and the garage with its enormous drums.
Say something that will strengthen me,
let me sip all the colas of the world
before I dive off this reef, into
that region of ferns and bubbles that awaits us,
where all are not so bright, but a few are.
These we clasp to us, our bodies' tattoos
seeking psychiatric help, and the earth
guzzles and slurps rhythmically.
A dog would like you for it,
but here no voice says to come all the way in.

Here are holdings,
taking name in the urban dusk
that grazed you just now. Have you brought the lesson?
Good, I was sure of it. But can no longer
go out past the doorman. Here, take this basket of iced cookies
anyway. And he jubilates. Everything is in time for him,
eating in the capacity, along with the French
and motorcycle community, is what the headphones told us.
And when we no longer have each other to look at
these buzz and resonate still. From what dark pitcher
or mirror I brought you, from Duluth, and minus
astral influences, you are grateful, and for wrappings in general.
It is time to feast
so soon again.

Slow crows still rally round that puncture mark
in a Danish heaven where a sawhorse delivers
the belated aspirin and spools are wound
in the interests of a greater clarity than this:

Soon, all will be hidden,
like a stage behind a red velvet curtain,
and this mole on your shoulder—no need to ask
it its name. In the brisk concealment
that has become general everything thrives:
bushes, lampposts, motels at the edge of airports
whose blue lights guide the descending vehicle
to a safe berth in soon-to-be night,
as wharves welcome their vessels, however frumpy
they may seem, with open arms.
And I think it says a lot about us, about
our welcoming, that days don't disturb themselves
or think too much about it, or manage
the disheveled trace that was to have been our signature.
We're too cagey for that in any case,
Wouldn't be fooled by the most elaborately duplicated passport,
bill of lading. It's as though we've come refreshed
from another planet, and spied immediately what was lacking in this one:
an orange, fresh linens, ink, a pen.

Still, the hothouse beckons.
I've told you before how afraid this makes me,
but I think we can handle it together,
and this is as good a place as any
to unseal my last surprise: you, as you go,
diffident, indifferent, but with the sky for an awning
for as many days as it pleases it to cover you.
That's what I meant by "get a handle," and as I say it,
both surface and subtext subside quintessentially
and the dead-letter office dissolves in the blue acquiescence of spring.

XIII.
You get hungry,
you eat hot.
Home's a cold delivery destination.
The emphatic nose puts it on hold.
Clubs are full.
I kind of like the all-night dust-up
though I'm sworn to secrecy,
with or without a cat.

I let so many people go by me
I sort of long for one of them, any
one, to turn back toward me,
forget these tears. As children we played at being grownups.
Now there's trouble brewing on the horizon.

So—if you want to come with me,
or just pull at my sleeve, let them make that discovery.
Summer won't end in your lap,
nor are the stars more casual than usual.
Peace, quiet, a dictionary—it was so important,
yet at the end nobody had any time for any of it.
It was as if all of it had never happened,
my shoelaces were untied, and—am I forgetting anything?

from CAN YOU HEAR, BIRD

(1995)

A POEM OF UNREST

Men duly understand the river of life,
misconstruing it, as it widens and its cities grow
dark and denser, always farther away.

And of course that remote denseness suits
us, as lambs and clover might have
if things had been built to order differently.

But since I don't understand myself, only segments
of myself that misunderstand each other, there's no
reason for you to want to, no way you could

even if we both wanted it. Do those towers even exist?
We must look at it that way, along those lines
so the thought can erect itself, like plywood battlements.

A WAKING DREAM

And the failing panopticon? That happened before,
when my uncle was in his bathrobe, on vacation.
Leastways, folks *said* it was a vacation . . .

Are you referring to your Uncle Obadiah,
the one that spent twenty years in the drunk-tank
and could whistle all the latest hits when sprung?
No one ever cared to talk much about it, it seemed a little *too*
peculiar, and he, he had forgotten the art
of knowing how far to go too far.

Just so. When driven, he would materialize in a Palm Beach suit
and Panama hat with tiny rainbow holes in it.
That was someone who knew how to keep up appearances
until he had exhausted them. Some of the railroad crew
got to know him at times, and could never figure out how he knew
exactly when a storm would hit. And when its anthracitic orgasm
erupted, we were out in the salley gardens mending coils
from the last big one. Such is my recollection. And vipers
would pause to notice. Meanwhile he was acting more and more

like a candidate. Then the wave of beach chairs crashed over us
and there was nothing more to be said for it. The case was closed,
it was "history," he liked to say, as though that were a topic
he could expand on if he chose, but it was more likely
to be night, and no one could extricate it properly.

Yet I had been told of an estimate.
That's what we don't know! If only I could get my senses
back in the right order, and had time to ponder this old message,
I could have the sluice-gates opened in a jiffy. As it is,
they're probably more than a little rusty, and do we know,
really know, as chasm-dwellers are said
to know, which way is upstream?

AT FIRST I THOUGHT I WOULDN'T
SAY ANYTHING ABOUT IT

but then I thought keeping quiet about it might appear even ruder.
At first I thought I had died and gone to heaven
but that scapegrace the unruly sun informed me otherwise.

I am in my heavyset pants and find this occupation of beekeeper charming
though I have yet to meet my first bee.
We don't know if I get to keep the hat and veil.

"Too hot," he said: "Too hot for everything!"
He so caring, so mundane. ". . . to have you on board."
Bulgarian choirs everywhere stood up and sang the song of the rent.
It was lovely. Now I shall take a short vacation,
proof that I am needed here. Nobody wants my two cents

anymore, I believe. To some it was like skating in summer.
A small turret perched over the lake. It exploded.
That's the way I feel about people taking me out
to some nice repast, and afterwards you go home and
go over everything that was stated. I prefer flowers and breathing.

A hears by chance a familiar name, and the name involves a riddle of the past.

B, in love with A, receives an unsigned letter in which the writer states that she is the mistress of A and begs B not to take him away from her.

B, compelled by circumstances to be a companion of A in an isolated place, alters her rosy views of love and marriage when she discovers, through A, the selfishness of men.

A, an intruder in a strange house, is discovered; he flees through the nearest door into a windowless closet and is trapped by a spring lock.

A is so content with what he has that any impulse toward enterprise is throttled.

A solves an important mystery when falling plaster reveals the place where some old love letters are concealed.

A-4, missing food from his larder, half believes it was taken by a "ghost."

A, a crook, seeks unlawful gain by selling A-8 an object, X, which A-8 already owns.

A sees a stranger, A-5, stealthily remove papers, X, from the pocket of another stranger, A-8, who is asleep. A follows A-5.

A sends an infernal machine, X, to his enemy, A-3, and it falls into the hands of A's friend, A-2.

Angela tells Philip of her husband's enlarged prostate, and asks for money.

Philip, ignorant of her request, has the money placed in an escrow account.

A discovers that his pal, W, is a girl masquerading as a boy.

A, discovering that W is a girl masquerading as a boy, keeps the knowledge to himself and does his utmost to save the masquerader from annoying experiences.

A, giving ten years of his life to a miserly uncle, U, in exchange for a college education, loses his ambition and enterprise.

A, undergoing a strange experience among a people weirdly deluded, discovers the secret of the delusion from Herschel, one of the victims who has died. By means of information obtained from the notebook, A succeeds in rescuing the other victims of the delusion.

A dies of psychic shock.

Albert has a dream, or an unusual experience, psychic or otherwise, which enables him to conquer a serious character weakness and become successful in his new narrative, "Boris Karloff."

[. . .]

Silver coins from the Mojave Desert turn up in the possession of a sinister jeweler.

Three musicians wager that one will win the affections of the local kapellmeister's wife; the losers must drown themselves in a nearby stream.

Ardis, caught in a trap and held powerless under a huge burning glass, is saved by an eclipse of the sun.

Kent has a dream so vivid that it seems a part of his waking experience.

A and A-2 meet with a tragic adventure, and A-2 is killed.

Elvira, seeking to unravel the mystery of a strange house in the hills, is caught in an electrical storm. During the storm the house vanishes and the site on which it stood becomes a lake.

Alphonse has a wound, a terrible psychic wound, an invisible psychic wound, which causes pain in flesh and tissue which, otherwise, are perfectly healthy and normal.

A has a dream which he conceives to be an actual experience.

Jenny, homeward bound, drives and drives, and is still driving, no nearer to her home than she was when she first started.

Petronius B. Furlong's friend, Morgan Windhover, receives a wound from which he dies.

Thirteen guests, unknown to one another, gather in a spooky house to hear Toe reading Buster's will.

Buster has left everything to Lydia, a beautiful Siamese girl poet of whom no one has heard.

Lassie and Rex tussle together politely; Lassie, wounded, is forced to limp home.

In the Mexican gold rush a city planner is found imprisoned by outlaws in a crude cage of sticks.

More people flow over the dam and more is learned about the missing electric cactus.

Too many passengers have piled onto a cable car in San Francisco; the conductor is obliged to push some of them off.

Maddalena, because of certain revelations she has received, firmly resolves that she will not carry out an enterprise that had formerly been dear to her heart.

Fog enters into the shaft of a coal mine in Wales.

A violent wind blows the fog around.

Two miners, Shawn and Hillary, are pursued by fumes.

Perhaps Emily's datebook holds the clue to the mystery of the seven swans under the upas tree.

Jarvis seeks to manage Emily's dress shop and place it on a paying basis. Jarvis's bibulous friend, Emily, influences Jarvis to take to drink, scoffing at the doctor who has forbidden Jarvis to indulge in spirituous liquors.

Jarvis, because of a disturbing experience, is compelled to turn against his friend, Emily.

A ham has his double, "Donnie," take his place in an important enterprise.

Jarvis loses his small fortune in trying to help a friend.

Lodovico's friend, Ambrosius, goes insane from eating the berries of a strange plant, and makes a murderous attack on Lodovico.

"New narrative" is judged seditious. Hogs from all over go squealing down the street.

Ambrosius, suffering misfortune, seeks happiness in the companionship of Joe, and in playing golf.

Arthur, in a city street, has a glimpse of Cathy, a strange woman who has caused him to become involved in a puzzling mystery.

Cathy, walking in the street, sees Arthur, a stranger, weeping.

Cathy abandons Arthur after he loses his money and is injured and sent to a hospital.

Arthur, married to Beatrice, is haunted by memories of a former sweetheart, Cornelia, a heartless coquette whom Alvin loves.

Sauntering in a park on a fine day in spring, Tricia and Plotinus encounter a little girl grabbing a rabbit by its ears. As they remonstrate with her, the girl is transformed into a mature woman who regrets her feverish act.

Running up to the girl, Alvin stumbles and loses his coins.

In a nearby dell, two murderers are plotting to execute a third.

Beatrice loved Alvin before he married.

B, second wife of A, discovers that B-3, A's first wife, was unfaithful.

B, wife of A, dons the mask and costume of B-3, A's paramour, and meets A as B-3; his memory returns and he forgets B-3, and goes back to B.

A discovers the "Hortensius," a lost dialogue of Cicero, and returns it to the crevice where it lay.

Ambrose marries Phyllis, a nice girl from another town.

Donnie and Charlene are among the guests invited to the window.

No one remembers old Everett, who is left to shrivel in a tower.

Pellegrino, a rough frontiersman in a rough frontier camp, undertakes to care for an orphan.

Ildebrando constructs a concealed trap, and a person near to him, Gwen, falls into the trap and cannot escape.

BY GUESS AND BY GOSH

Even so, we have forgotten their graves.
I swear to you I will not beat one drum in your absence.

And the beasts of night will not forget their crimes,
nor the others their roly-polyness.

It was in a garage where tire irons jangled in the breeze
to the accompaniment of flyswatters functioning
that we first heard of that Phoenician sailor
and how when the tide was out he would pretend to be
the Flying Dutchman on one of his infrequent shore leaves
to garner a spouse. But he was all red with jewels—
not rubies, cheap gems. And his incisors struck fear
in the hearts of the entourage. Nevertheless, many
were the maidens who considered him an option,
though they always ended by rejecting it. Some said it was his breath,
others, the driven cornsilk of his hair. Perhaps
it was the lack of something called "personable,"
though I think I don't even want to know what that is, I'll follow
my heart over warm oceans of Chinese lounge music
until the day the badger coughs up that secret,
though first we must discover the emetic,
the one I told you about.

Confused minions swarmed on the quarterdeck.
No one was giving orders anymore. In fact it was quite a while
since any had been issued. Who's in charge here?
Can't anyone stop the player piano before it rolls us
in the trough of a tidal wave? How did we get to be so many?
I wonder what's playing at the local movie theater.
Some Hitchcock or other, for there are many fanciers
in these unsightly parts. And who would want mothers
for supper?

CAN YOU HEAR, BIRD

And for all the days it doesn't happen
something does happen,
solid and nutritional like a wrapped steak
tossed on a counter. At first I couldn't believe the thirst;

soon, so soon, it becomes average and airy,
a fixture. Precept to be toyed with.
The road started to get rough with me.
A mere 800 feet away the car wept
on its blocks
and little Peter came and looked around and went away.

It was kind of a mistake and he went away.

It was a kind mistake, breezes over dashboard.
Twin violins sew
a fine seam;
a paw slips over the face of the clock,
laggards and dudgeons in between.

All I meant to suggest was the negative of what has
been done surges and slops against fifth-floor windows
in the time it takes to anchor a tricycle.
And we full of such courtesy,
blind to the days and it seems their systems the night,
teetering on a board's edge;
sure and the unrolled film fans out
in suns like a dolphin or a skate's wing.
After all who blubbered the truth
It wasn't I

CANTILEVER

I knew we should have stopped back there
by the pudding station
but the pudding people were so—well—
full of themselves.

The Sphinx didn't want us to come this far
even though we answered her questions
and threw in a bonus answer: "As honey is to the jaguar."

And we so well all along too—

Coming up is the world's longest single cantilever span.
I am numb with thrips.

He was a soldier or a Shaker. At least he was doing *something*,
going somewhere. Often, in the evenings, he'd rant about Mark Twain,
how that wasn't his real name, and was he hiding something?
If so, then why call himself a humorist?
We began to tire of his ravings, but (as so often happens)
it was just at that point that a salient character trait
revealed itself, or rather, manifested itself within him.
It was one of those goofy days in August
when all men (and some women) dream of chocolate sodas.
He confessed he'd had one for lunch,
then took us out to the street to show us the whir and dazzle
of living in some other city, where so much that is different goes on.
I guess he was inspired by Lahore. Said it came to him
in his dreams every night. And little by little
we felt ourselves being transported there. Not that we wanted
to be there, far from that. But we were either too timid
or unaware to urge him otherwise. Then he mentioned Timbuktu.
Said he'd actually been there, that the sidewalks were pink
and the huts made of mother-of-pearl, not mud, as is commonly
supposed. Said he'd had the best venison and apple tart
in his life there.
       Well, we were accompanying him in the daze
that usually surrounded him, when we began to think about ourselves:
When *was* the last time we had done so? And the stranger shifted shape
again (he was now wearing a Zouave's culottes), and asked us
would we want to *live* in Djibouti, or Providence, or Lyon, now that
we'd seen them, and we chorused (like frogs), Oh no, we
want to live in New York, not that the other places aren't as splendid
and interesting as you say. It's just that New York
feels more like home to us. It's ugly, it's dirty, the people are rude

(kind and rude), and every surface has a fine film of filth
on it that behooves slobs like us, and will in time turn to diamonds,
just like the mother-of-pearl shacks in Timbuktu. And he said,
You know I was wrong about Mark Twain. It was his real name,
and he was a humorist, a genuine American humorist for the ages.

Of course you will. It happens even after you're dead.
Or, in some cases, the results are positive, but the verdict
negative. "In such a muddle," you said, and "all muddled up."
I wish I could help but I've a million things to do
and restoring your peace of mind isn't one of them. There goes my phone . . .

The professor's opinion on all this was: "Well, he leaps around,
doesn't he, your little surgeon-poet. Seems to lead an agitated life
on the surface, but if you really listen to him you find he's got
everything down pat. Knows where his bread is buttered, and his ass.
I could open a drawer of rhetorical footnotes, translated from
the Japanese or Old Church Slavonic, if I felt like it, and in there'd
be something that rhymes with him and his coziness, his following the trail
all the way back to its point of origin. Plus his lively friendliness, which
coexists, numinously I grant, with a desire to inflict harm.

There is a poetry in mere existence,
the kind that shopkeepers and people walking along the street lead,
you know, and evenness, that fills them up to whatever brim
is there, and stays, transient, all the days of their lives.
Such enharmonics are not for your poet-person. He sees, and breeds:
Otherwise the game isn't worth the candle to him. He'd as soon rhyme breeze
with breathes, as walk over to that fire hydrant in the grass
to examine it, see what it's made of, make sure it's not an idea in some
philosopher's mind, that will bruise and cloud over once that mind's
removed, leaving but a dubious trace of itself, like a ring of puffball dust . . . "

Suppose we grant its power of conserving to listening,
so it's really a full-fledged element in the creative process.
Well, others have done just that from time immemorial,
when women wore tall cones on their heads with sails attached to them.
But, as mattering ages, it hardens into something smooth like good luck,

no longer kinetic. Then you can listen all you want
at palace doors, creaky vents . . .

This imploring process is twofold. First, let's not forget its root
in implosive. That's something it's got up its sleeve.
Did you ever see an anarchist without his round bomb?
And then the someone that's got to be implored,
how does he fit in? I'll tell you: like a wedge that was subtracted
from a wheel of cheese, and is replaced, so that it fits perfectly;
no one can see where the cut was. Well, that's
poetic argument for you. It stands on its own ("The cheese stands alone"),
but can at the drop of a speculation be seen again as a part,
a vital one, of the mucus cloud that is generalized human thought aimed at
a quarrel or a rebus in the lining. And that's the way
we get old with poetry. Comes a time when no one has a notion
of anything else, and the odor of fried brains contends
with the damp of vacant ancestral halls, to their mutual
betterment, actually. Here, hand me that cod . . .

DEBIT NIGHT

We were coming down from the city the city is where you come when you don't want to listen or be excused from listening. It is a hard hat out and some days "stiletto" heels—but who told you about hat we don't know about hat too much or about how "hat" grows. Coming down we passed through a former violet producing center. Around World War I there were maybe a hundred violet farms in this region of New York state conducive to violets. It is a very labor intensive thing now there are no longer any except one or two. Up until the end of World War II it was the fashion for ladies to wear bunches of violets but then

it changed. Now no one had any use for them. Now everyone likes violets I don't see. Yes but you don't see anybody wearing them or buying any. Some even think of them as weeds. Nevertheless the former violet business has left its trace in place-names here such as Violet Lane and Violet Hill. They are beautiful aren't they until you stop to think that violets could be weeds and of a reason why nobody buys them anymore. Yes but I will still think the

names

A sandbox sometimes had weeds growing in it including one that looked like a dandelion only it was tall and thrifty. Always was the sand more beautiful after the rain when there was a dried wet crust on top with pebblelike pores starring its surface. But mostly it was out of sight. There was not a window of the house where it wasn't around the corner so naturally it is seen less and thus gets worn into the mind like a crease in a road map that has been folded up the wrong way too many times.

Jana prefers the city. Says there's more light in it, or the light gets divided up by the streets more so a little goes a long way. Light is something that should not be wasted so as to produce its maximum effect as it is even on some boulevards where it stretches out too much, too wide and too long into the future. This is true but in the country it gets more soaked up in the bushes and buildings so a little more is always required and a little more is all there is. In the city you can eavesdrop on brick walls and this is called "repointing." What comes up in the inevitable ensuing conversation is sure funny but doesn't look ahead to the future of philosophy or decide how life should ultimately be lived. There is no conversation even about half-serious things like the theater. Instead everybody makes a unique little mess like a child shitting in its pants that's proud of it. The auto horns scare everything near away anyhow. The place pivots; this has already been patented. You can go down to sleep by the river or in a movie. See that boat? It's real.

So after we had done the chores and brought back living to the house there was something on its mind like a ball of yarn. Yes, a ball of yarn is what is there as I wanted to say. Say, stay anyway will you? I might. I've got things to do. Yes, but this is one of them. That's true. But I still have things to do I might go. Oh no you're not. Oh no? Okay then I really will stay because I want to really. Really she said? Then I will show you this dried crust of bread which is the truth, you must never forget it. Oh I never will I said it's what I wanted all along. How many acres do you want? Oh I never sought them they always came to me until quite recently. Indeed? Well here comes another one it's green or black. It must be yours she said. You played the mandrake right. Yes well here comes another and a whole lot of them. By George she said we should have been ready for them, but that's the way

it is you can't be and you are. Think of World War I, it's green and black and surely there was less daylight around then, more fog and boats on the East River with people lining up to go on them. Yes it was a premonition of these our times she said and so I conjure you, don't go around telling what you know to people, you are likely to get it back. Then peace, of a sort? The high-minded sun combs the tallest man-made structures on earth and then you get a little peace and some darkness down in the lobbies where everything begins to happen. No one in his handsome and enduring stable. Just having to endure is like going for the jugular but it should be a caravanserai. The problem is to get over what is being endured but hasn't been and to make for the middle distance, after the teacups and primulas but before philosophy and "last things," where thighs shine astride dim neighboring curbs and strangers greet you convulsively. These are more last things, I think, to think about

all along along what I wanted all along

DULL MAUVE

Twenty miles away, in the colder
waters of the Atlantic, you gaze longingly
toward the coast. Didn't you once love someone
there? Yes, but it was only a cat, and I,
a manatee, what could I do? There are no rewards
in this world for pissing your life away, even
if it means you get to see forgotten icebergs
of decades ago peeling off from the mass
to dive under the surface, raising a
mountain of seething glass before they lunge back up
to start the unknown perilous journey
to the desolate horizon.

                    That was the way
I thought of each day when I was young, a sloughing-off,
both suicidal and imbued with a certain ritual grace.
Later, there were so many protagonists
one got quite lost, as in a forest of doppelgängers.
Many things were going on. And the moon, poised
on the ridge like an enormous, smooth grapefruit, understood
the importance of each and wasn't going
to make one's task any easier, though we loved her.

Just when I thought there wasn't room enough
for another thought in my head, I had this great idea—
call it a philosophy of life, if you will. Briefly,
it involved living the way philosophers live,
according to a set of principles. OK, but which ones?

That was the hardest part, I admit, but I had a
kind of dark foreknowledge of what it would be like.
Everything, from eating watermelon or going to the bathroom
or just standing on a subway platform, lost in thought
for a few minutes, or worrying about rain forests,
would be affected, or more precisely, inflected
by my new attitude. I wouldn't be preachy,
or worry about children and old people, except
in the general way prescribed by our clockwork universe.
Instead I'd sort of let things be what they are
while injecting them with the serum of the new moral climate
I thought I'd stumbled into, as a stranger
accidentally presses against a panel and a bookcase slides back,
revealing a winding staircase with greenish light
somewhere down below, and he automatically steps inside
and the bookcase slides shut, as is customary on such occasions.
At once a fragrance overwhelms him—not saffron, not lavender,
but something in between. He thinks of cushions, like the one
his uncle's Boston bull terrier used to lie on watching him
quizzically, pointed ear-tips folded over. And then the great rush
is on. Not a single idea emerges from it. It's enough
to disgust you with thought. But then you remember something William James
wrote in some book of his you never read—it was fine, it had the fineness,
the powder of life dusted over it, by chance, of course, yet still looking
for evidence of fingerprints. Someone had handled it
even before he formulated it, though the thought was his and his alone.

      [. . .]

It's fine, in summer, to visit the seashore.
There are lots of little trips to be made.
A grove of fledgling aspens welcomes the traveler. Nearby
are the public toilets where weary pilgrims have carved
their names and addresses, and perhaps messages as well,
messages to the world, as they sat
and thought about what they'd do after using the toilet
and washing their hands at the sink, prior to stepping out
into the open again. Had they been coaxed in by principles,
and were their words philosophy, of however crude a sort?
I confess I can move no further along this train of thought—
something's blocking it. Something I'm
not big enough to see over. Or maybe I'm frankly scared.
What was the matter with how I acted before?
But maybe I can come up with a compromise—I'll let
things be what they are, sort of. In the autumn I'll put up jellies
and preserves, against the winter cold and futility,
and that will be a human thing, and intelligent as well.
I won't be embarrassed by my friends' dumb remarks,
or even my own, though admittedly that's the hardest part,
as when you are in a crowded theater and something you say
riles the spectator in front of you, who doesn't even like the idea
of two people near him talking together. Well he's
got to be flushed out so the hunters can have a crack at him—
this thing works both ways, you know. You can't always
be worrying about others and keeping track of yourself
at the same time. That would be abusive, and about as much fun
as attending the wedding of two people you don't know.
Still, there's a lot of fun to be had in the gaps between ideas.
That's what they're made for! Now I want you to go out there
and enjoy yourself, and yes, enjoy your philosophy of life, too.
They don't come along every day. Look out! There's a big one . . .

It is true that I can no longer remember very well
the time when we first began to know each other.
However, I do remember very well
the first time we met. You walked in sunlight,
holding a daisy. You said, "Children make unreliable witnesses."

Now, so long after that time,
I keep the spirit of it throbbing still.
The ideas are still the same, and they expand
to fill vast, antique cubes.

My daughter was reading one just the other day.
She said, "How like pellucid statues, Daddy. Or like a . . .
an engine."

In this house of blues the cold creeps stealthily upon us.
I do not dare to do what I fantasize doing.
With time the blue congeals into roomlike purple
that takes the shape of alcoves, landings . . .
Everything is like something else.
I should have waited before I learned this.

OPERATORS ARE STANDING BY

In some of the stores they sell a cheese rinse
for disturbed or depressed hair. You add whiskey
to it at the last moment. Now that
it's nearly Christmas, we could buy
such things, you and I, and take them with us,
though it seems like
only yesterday I hit that Halloween homerun.
It backed up and kind of flowed back
into my side I think, creating a "strawberry
jar" effect. There was nothing Arvin
or I could do about it.

Determining everyone is a bigshot
is sometimes all he cares about.
I've slept on the ground with him,
and deep in a birchbark canoe.
Once there was two of him.
At school no one could tell us apart
until we smiled, or his big laugh came unbuttoned.
Fatally, venery has taken its toll
of him these last years. I can't
get near him without being reminded of Venus,
or the hunt. I come in six different packages,
from the "jewel case" to Wrigley's spearmint.
In the time of friendly moose
droppings I followed them to the Shedd Aquarium.
No one was selling tickets that day.
I wandered in and out of the fish tanks,
stopping occasionally to leave a handprint
on the plate glass for the benefit of some fish or other.

PLAIN AS DAY

with all its accoutrements
(of course)—intact, impervious
to air, sand, and time—the three fatal
sisters with nary a thought
in their heads except where to cut it—
and it goes out, like a candle or a father
to buy a pack of cigarettes. You knew
this. WE all knew it. It's the old

weather shuffle behind a different
sun veil—shot, diapered
the way they always want it.

It never snows on Tuesday—far
be it from me to suggest otherwise, only
there *is* this difference, this little difference
that won't go away,
that's been waiting since before the office opened.
What shall I tell it?

Those that are taken leave no footprint
on the air, no smile
on the soused sky.
It's another kind of smile
speeding toward us like an express train
we'll never see. Please put out the light,
the ashes, when you leave.

Same in Texas or Louisiana. Meaning
no mail for you today, and would you please call back?
It's urgent. Well, *was*. I've been waiting hours
on a bench next to a fugitive general.

[. . .]

"Be sure of retail," he says. "The life insurance building, the pickle garden. Heaven knows they attack our radar too, swoop down on us like bats and the mystery illness."

Are you Big Bang?

Cervantes was asleep when he wrote *Don Quixote*.

Joyce slept during the Wandering Rocks section of *Ulysses*.

Homer nodded and occasionally slept during the greater part of the *Iliad*; he was awake however when he wrote the *Odyssey*.

Proust snored his way through *The Captive*, as have legions of his readers after him.

Melville was asleep at the wheel for much of *Moby-Dick*.

Fitzgerald slept through *Tender Is the Night*, which is perhaps not so surprising,

but the fact that Mann slumbered on the very slopes of *The Magic Mountain* is quite extraordinary—that he wrote it, even more so.

Kafka, of course, never slept, even while not writing or on bank holidays.

No one knows too much about George Eliot's writing habits—my guess is she would sleep a few minutes, wake up and write something, then pop back to sleep again.

Lew Wallace's forty winks came, incredibly, during the chariot race in *Ben-Hur*.

Emily Dickinson slept on her cold, narrow bed in Amherst.

When she awoke there would be a new poem inscribed by Jack Frost on the windowpane; outside, glass foliage chimed.

Good old Walt snored as he wrote and, like so many of us, insisted he didn't.

Maugham snored on the Riviera.

Agatha Christie slept daintily, as a woman sleeps, which is why her novels are like tea sandwiches—artistic, for the most part.

I sleep when I cannot avoid it; my writing and sleeping are constantly improving.

I have other things to say, but shall not detain you much.

Never go out in a boat with an author—they cannot tell when they are over water.

Birds make poor role models.

A philosopher should be shown the door, but don't, under any circumstances, try it.

Slaves make good servants.

Brushing the teeth may not always improve the appearance.

Store clean rags in old pillow cases.

Feed a dog only when he barks.

Flush tea leaves down the toilet, coffee grounds down the sink.

Beware of anonymous letters—you may have written them, in a wordless implosion of sleep.

THE FAINT OF HEART

were always right
about things like chansons de geste
and why they couldn't, at the time, be bothered.
Huon de Bordeaux was a highly important person
at least in Bordeaux which is an important French city,
that smells better than Perth Amboy but worse than Newton-le-Willows.
As has been pointed out
by myself and by other researchers, the object of the game
is to sit on a cold rattle.

I love the broad avenues of Washington, D.C.,
all leading toward—what? What is it they are escaping from?
Who in this great city cares anything about these data
that are the wellspring of truth? Torches emblazon the field
in front of the White House, which is where our president sits,
and Congress, when it is in session. Have I omitted anybody?
No, only the man who summons the president's taxi
who is too unimportant to figure in your list.
What about that dray horse's withers? Ah,
I shall have to begin again,
to start all over again from the beginning. Nomenclature
being its own reward.

And the fang? It's pleasant-looking and practical.
The board of surveyors is ours.
I trust in and admire it.
The Bureau of Mines belongs to all of us
in this dang-blasted country. Each of us has a share in tomorrow.
The light on that ilex
reminds me of an old school-chum of mine. None of us,
you see, was ever divested of anything,
which is why we're running riot now, in the alphabet-coded streets
and others named in memory of hydrangeas and vernal blushes.

And he said, "Varnish the floor!"
Winter is coming and it's going to be spectacular.
The squirrels and woolly caterpillars told me so.

In time the review squads appeared.
They carried Gatlings and were dressed in plum-colored eighteenth-century uniforms.
The mood was sour. I offered to chase a member of the enemy
but it wasn't going down well. Then *you* appeared, covered
with rubies, and it was decided we should "get down."
Secaucus had looked better. The snow on the reeds—

Soon the president joined us. He was worried but polite.
The daughters in their simple white frocks came out on the White House lawn
and had a very nice chat. They said it was an allegory
or oligarchy, and to roll with the punches. Better
alive and upbraided than rocked in the cradle of the deep,
someone said. But that's what I'm trying to oppose—
how you been?

THE GREEN MUMMIES

Avuncular and teeming, the kind luggage
hosed down the original site. Who is ready
last, but I kind of get a kick
out of what-the-heck's surface optimism.
He doesn't believe in sex—that's *one* point
in his favor—but knows all the standard
Antonio stories and has told them to the Ladies'
Auxiliary in Loophole. You see, all his life
he wanted to be a trainer, or *something,* maggots
even. But fate's crow-like wing
had other plans for him. We were meant to have slept
during the time we were awake and learning; conversely,
as air-raid wardens we made good Michelin men—the tummy
always in repose, the chin barely protected by a ruff
of sneering blight. But it's time

you took that old comforter off. Adam and Eve
on a raft could say good day here, laughter in the
loved opus sounding. Yet wan derision only
watches, won't come forward. Next year is electric;
this one only divides and serves us, bathes us,
as we know how. Better pickled moray
than a jungle diorama, full of who-knows-what quirks
and surfaces. Yet I like him; his white hat
fell off and landed in the sound. Mortified,
he herded us into the vestibule; we had brought
the wrong kind of medlars.

THE MILITARY BASE

Now, in summer, the handiwork of spring
is all around us. What did we think those
tendrils were for, except to go on growing
some more, and then collapse, totally
disinterested. "Uninterested" is probably
what I should say, but they seem to like it here.
At any rate, their secret says so,
like a B-flat clarinet under the arches
of some grove.

The house took a direct hit
but it didn't matter; the next moment
it was intact, though transparent.
No injuries were reported.
There were no reports of looting
or insane buggery behind altars.

THE PROBLEM OF ANXIETY

Fifty years have passed
since I started living in those dark towns
I was telling you about.
Well, not much has changed. I still can't figure out
how to get from the post office to the swings in the park.
Apple trees blossom in the cold, not from conviction,
and my hair is the color of dandelion fluff.

Suppose this poem were about you—would *you*
put in the things I've carefully left out:
descriptions of pain, and sex, and how shiftily
people behave toward each other? Naw, that's
all in some book it seems. For you
I've saved the descriptions of chicken sandwiches,
and the glass eye that stares at me in amazement
from the bronze mantel, and will never be appeased.

TODAY'S ACADEMICIANS

Again, what forces the critic to bury his
agenda in interleaving textualities and so
bring the past face-to-face with his present
isn't naughty, but it *is* both silly and wrong.
The past will have to get by on sheer pluck
or charm, entirely consistent with its ten-
dency to nullify and romanticize things. The
way a pain begins. The flying squirrels of
this particular rain forest mope in flight;
the audience has already done what it can for
them; and the pure light of their endeavor
bespeaks the modesty of the program: "mere?"
anarchy. That the men with spotted suits
and ties get down to it is one more nail in
their coffin. These portly curmudgeons dig-
nify no endeavor and are also about as "right"
as the weather ever gets. All in my time.
More meteor magic. Seems like.

from TUESDAY EVENING

We see one thing next to another. In time they get superimposed
and then who looks silly? Not us, as you might think, but the curve
we are plotted on, head to head, a parabola in the throes
of vomiting its formula, piqued by the sullen verve

of day, while night is siphoned off again. And as wolverines
prefer Michigan, so this civil branch of holly is nailed to your door, lest you
fear my coming, or any uncivil declaiming, or submarines
in the bay that spreads out before us, or any gumshoe.

We'll party when the millennium gets closer. Meanwhile
I wanted to mention your feet. A dowser
could locate your contentedness zone. But where have you been while
folk dancing broke out, and colorful piñatas, waking Bowser

in his kennel, rendering the last victuals
in the larder unappetizing? Yet those feet shall impose the glory
of my slogans on the unsuspecting world that belittles
them now, but shall whistle them *con amore*

anon. That doesn't mean "peace at any price,"
but a shaking-down of old, purblind principles
that were always getting in the way. Self-sacrifice
will be on the agenda, a lowering of expectations, a ban on municipal

iron fences and picnics. Man must return to his earth,
experience its seasons, frosts, its labyrinthine
processes, the spectacle of continual rebirth
in one's own time. Only then will the sunshine

each weekday lodges in its quiver expand till the vernal
equinox rounds it off, then subtracts a little more each day,
though always leaving a little, even in hyperboreal climes where eternal
ice floes fringe the latitudes. On a beautiful day in May

[. . .]

you might forget this, but there it is, always creeping up on you.
Permit me then for the umpteenth time to reiterate
that basking in the sun like an otter or curlew
isn't the whole story. Tomorrow may obliterate

your projects and belongings, casting a shadow longer than the equator
into your private sector, to wit, your plan to take a Hovercraft
across the lagoon and have lunch there, leaving the waiter
a handsome tip. For though your garrison be fully staffed,

the near future, like an overcrowded howdah,
trumpets its imminent arrival, opens the floodgate
of a thousand teeming minor ills, spoiling the chowder
and marching society's annual gymkhana, letting in smog to asphyxiate

palms and eucalyptuses. One paddles in the backwash of the present,
laughing at its doodles, unpinning its robes,
smoothing its ribbons, and lo and behold an unpleasant
emu is blocking the path; its one good eye probes

your premises and tacit understandings, and the outing
is postponed till another day. Or you could be reclining
on a rock, like Fra Diavolo, and have it sneak up on you, spouting
praise for the way the city looks after a shower, divining

its outer shallows from the number of storm windows
taken down and stashed away, for it has the shape of a sonata—
bent, unyielding. And, once it's laid out in windrows,
open to the difficult past, that of a fish on a platter.

    [. . .]

Expect no malice from it and freshets
will foam, gathering strength as they leapfrog the mountain.
But a quieter realism plumbs the essence of ponds, as nitwits
worship the machine-tooled elegies of the fountain,

that wets its basin and the nearby grass. In a moment the dustmen
will be here, and in the time remaining it behooves
me to insist again on the lust men
invent, then cherish. But since my mistress disapproves,

I'll toe the line. And should you ask me why, sir,
I'll say it's because one's sex drives are like compulsive handwashing:
better early on in life than late. Yet I'm still spry, sir,
though perhaps no longer as dashing

as in times gone by, and can wolf down the elemental
in one gulp—its "How different one feels after doing something:
calm, and in a calm way almost tragic; in any case far from the ungentle
figure we cut in the reveries of others, a rum thing

not fit to be seen in public with." Yet it is this ominous bedouin
whose contours blur when someone glimpses
us, that is what we are remembered as, for no one can see our genuine
side falling to pieces all down our declamatory gestures. They treat pimps as

equals, ignoring all shortcomings save ours. And of course, no commerce
is possible between these two noncommunicating vessels of our being. As urushiol
is to poison ivy, so is our own positive self-image the obverse
of all that will ever be said and thought about us, the vitriol

[. . .]

we gargle with in the morning, just as others do. This impasse
does, however, have an escape clause written into it: planned
enhancements, they call it. So that if one *is* knocked flat on his ass
by vile opprobrium, he need only consult his pocket mirror: The sand

will seem to flow upward through the hourglass; one is pickled
in one's own humors, yet the dismantled ideal
rescued from youth is still pulsing, viable, having trickled
from the retort of self-consciousness into the frosted vial

of everyone's individual consciousness noting it's the same
as all the others, with one vital difference: It belongs to no one.
Thus a few may climb several steps above the crowd, achieve fame
and personal fulfillment in a flaring instant, sing songs to one

more beloved than the rest, yet still cherish the charm and quirkiness
that entangle all individuals in the racemes
of an ever-expanding Sargasso Sea whose murkiness
comes at last to seem exemplary. So, between two extremes

hidden in blue distance, the dimensionless
regions of the self do have their day. We like this, that,
and the other; have our doubts about certain things; enjoy pretension less
than we did when we were young; are not above throwing out a caveat

or two; and in a word are comfortable in the saddle
reality offers to each of her children, simultaneously
convincing each of us we're superior, that no one else could straddle
her mount as elegantly as we. And when, all extraneously,

    [. . .]

the truth erupts, and we find we are but one of an army of supernumeraries
raising spears to salute the final duet
between our ego and the endlessly branching itineraries
of our *semblables*, a robed celebrant is already lifting the cruet

of salve to anoint the whole syndrome. And it's their proper
perspective that finally gets clamped onto things and us, including
our attitudes, hopes, half-baked ambitions, psychoses: everything an eavesdropper
already knows about us, along with the clothes we wear and the brooding

interiors we inhabit. It's getting late; the pageant
oozes forward, act four is yet to come, and so is dusk.
Still, ripeness must soon be intuited; a coolant
freeze the tragic act under construction. Let's husk

the ear of its plenitude, forget additional worries,
let Mom and apple pie go down the tubes, if indeed
that's their resolve. For, satisfying as it is to fling a pot, once the slurry's
reached the proper consistency, better still is it to join the stampede

away from it once it's finished. Which, as of now,
it is. Wait a minute! You told us eternal flux
was the ordering principle here, and in the next breath you disavow
open-endedness. What kind of clucks

do you take us for, anyway? Everyone knows that once something's finished,
decay sets in. But we were going to outwit all that. So
where's your panacea now? The snake oil? Smoke and mirrors? Diminished
expectations can never supplant the still-moist, half-hesitant tableau

    [. . .]

we thought to be included in, and to pursue
our private interests and destinies in, till doomsday. Well, I
never said my system was foolproof. You did too! I did not. Did too!
Did not. Did too. Did not. Did too. Hell, I

only said let's wait awhile and see what happens, maybe
something will, and if it doesn't, well, our personal
investment in the thing hasn't been that enormous, you crybaby;
we can still emerge unscathed. These are exceptional

times, after all. And all along I thought I was pointed
in the right direction, that if I just kept my seat
I'd get to a destination. I knew the instructions were disjointed,
garbled, but imagined we'd eventually make up the lost time. Yet one deadbeat

can pollute a whole universe. The sensuous green mounds
I'd been anticipating are nowhere to be seen. Instead, a dull
urban waste reveals itself, vistas of broken masonry, out of bounds
to the ordinary time traveler. How, then, did he lull

us, me and the others, into signing on for the trip?
By exposing himself, and pretending
not to see. Solar wind sandpapers the airstrip,
while only a few hundred yards away, bending

hostesses coddle stranded voyagers with canapés
and rum punch. To have had this in the early stage,
not the earliest, but the one right after the days
began to shorten imperceptibly! And one's rage

[. . .]

was a good thing, good for oneself and even
for others, at that critical juncture. Dryness
of the mouth was seldom a problem. Winking asides would leaven
the dullest textbook. Your highness

knows all this, yet if she will but indulge
my wobbling fancies a bit longer, I'll . . . Where was I? Oh, and then
a great hurricane came, and took away the leaves. The bulge
in the calceolaria bush was gone. By all the gods, when

next I saw him, he was gay, gay as any jackanapes. Is
this really what you had in mind, I asked.
But he merely smiled and replied, "None of your biz,"
and walked out onto the little peninsula and basked

as though he meant it. And in a funny kind of way, the nifty
feeling of those years has returned. I can't explain it,
but perhaps it means that once you're over fifty
you're rid of a lot of decibels. You've got a tiger; so unchain it

and then see what explanations they give. Walk through
your foot to the place behind it, the air
will frizz your whiskers. You're still young enough to talk through
the night, among friends, the way you used to do somewhere.

An alphabet is forming words. We who watch them
never imagine pronouncing them, and another opportunity
is missed. You must be awake to snatch them—
them, and the scent they give off with impunity.

    [. . .]

We all tagged along, and in the end there was nothing
to see—nothing and a lot. A lot in terms of contour, texture,
world. That sort of thing. The real fun and its clothing.
You can forget that. Next, you're

planning a brief trip. Perhaps a visit to Paul Bunyan
and Babe, the blue ox. There's time now. Piranhas
dream, at peace with themselves and with the floating world. A grunion
slips nervously past. The heat, the stillness are oppressive. Iguanas . . .

YES, DR. GRENZMER. HOW MAY I BE OF
ASSISTANCE TO YOU? WHAT! YOU SAY
THE PATIENT HAS ESCAPED?

We were staying at the Golden Something-or-Other.
Anyway, what does it matter now?
The boats have rolled up their colored sails.
The city is like a hinge. In the morning its glass
girders are flushed with light that gets drained
in the afternoon, but then something funny happens:
The westward-looking buildings reflect the sun's
rays more fiercely than they are projected.
They become a rival sunset in the east. That's heresy,
or at any rate bigamy. Tall buildings
"to suckle fools and chronicle small beer"; such is my story,
but I'm glad to be having this chance to tell it to you
even though we are in a silent movie and can speak only words
painted with milk. Yet someone comes to care about them:
There is always someone to care, somewhere,

but the sheriff vandalizes the day they return.
I didn't let you dream about it.
It is for this I am being punished
by reforms harder than the ones in Congress.
They have rules to go by, sins to atone for:
I, I have only weightlessness
and a vague feeling that I should be spending my time
doing other things—sweeping the apartment,
washing out a child's mouth with soap.

It was nugatory. They fed us delicacies
while we waited for the order of quilts to arrive—
or was it kilts? Joshua had this haunted feeling
he'd never finalized it at the start, when all

should have been beginning, but instead was pleased to slosh around
in mid-harbor. Anyway, there *were* invoices. Of that
he was almost certain. And a number of young girls
came and stood around the tree in which he was sitting—
were *they* the ones who had placed orders for the kilts?
Or were they mere raisin fanciers? "You'll see
when the weather gets dry and yellow the raisins
will form all by themselves, alone on the branches,
and no one will care. And those that like to eat them
real fast out of boxes won't have a clue
as to why that old horse-collar is draped over a branch
of the weeping willow, causing it to weep (that is,
bestir its leaves) even harder. Some people somewhere are prepared
for a few things to happen, but that's not counting us or our
immediate families. An apple-green boxcar slithers along
a distant railway, yearning for something
unnameable at the end of the canyon. Not
a handful of raisins, probably, but you catch my drift."

Soon all was drift. They had a feeling
they had better go inside, yet none could make a move
in that direction. All remained transfixed. "Tell them,"
the skald continued, "but only if they ask,
how this situation came about. We'll see then
what jury will convict me, just because I feel like a woman
trapped in a man's body, but only a little—not enough
to want to wear a skirt, but enough
to make me feel like putting on a kilt, and even then
only in Scotland, if I should be so lucky
as to find myself there some day." Tremors
stirred the little band; there was obvious sympathy
for his plight, mingled with something more acidulous,

like pickling spices. And all the girls turned away
to weep, but were changed to ivy
and stuff like that. Why am I telling you this?
To assuage my conscience, perhaps, hoping the bad dreams
will go away, or at least become more liberally mixed
with the good, for none are totally good
or bad, just like the people who keep walking into them,
and the scenery, familiar or obvious though it be.

Besides, I've raised one major issue—
at least credit me with that. It will be a long time
before this turns to nothing, and in the meantime
we can sit upon the ground, and tell sad stories
of the lives of pets, as the ground freezes and thaws
many times—it is past caring. And what goes on within us
will be inscribed by the dancing needle on our chart,
for others to consult and be derived from.
I thought it would all end casually on a bank
of flowers, but alas, a real bank was growing out of it,
with tellers and guards. Who liked the flowers.

YOU WOULD HAVE THOUGHT

Meanwhile, back in
soulless America, people are having fun
as usual.

A bird visits a birdbath.
A young girl takes a refresher course
in polyhistory. My mega-units are straining
at the leash of spring.
The annual race is on—

white flowers in someone's hair.
He comes in waltzing on empty airs,

mulling the blue notes of your case.
The leash is elastic and receptive
but I fear I am too wrapped up in cloudlets
of my own making this time.

In the other time it was rain dripping
from a tree to a house to the ground—
each thing helping itself and another thing
along a little. That would be inconceivable
these days of receptive answers and aggressive querying.

The routine is all too familiar,

the stone path wearying.

from WAKEFULNESS

(1998)

WAKEFULNESS

An immodest little white wine, some scattered seraphs,
recollections of the Fall—tell me,
has anyone made a spongier representation, chased
fewer demons out of the parking lot
where we all held hands?

Little by little the idea of the true way returned to me.
I was touched by your care,
reduced to fawning excuses.
Everything was spotless in the little house of our desire,
the clock ticked on and on, happy about
being apprenticed to eternity. A gavotte of dust-motes
came to replace my seeing. Everything was as though
it had happened long ago
in ancient peach-colored funny papers
wherein the law of true opposites was ordained
casually. Then the book opened by itself
and read to us: "You pack of liars,
of course tempted by the crossroads, but I like each
and every one of you with a peculiar sapphire intensity.
Look, here is where I failed at first.
The client leaves. History goes on and on,
rolling distractedly on these shores. Each day, dawn
condenses like a very large star, bakes no bread,
shoes the faithless. How convenient if it's a dream."

In the next sleeping car was madness.
An urgent languor installed itself
as far as the cabbage-hemmed horizons. And if I put a little
bit of myself in this time, stoppered the liquor that is our selves'
truant exchanges, brandished my intentions
for once? But only I get

something out of this memory.
A kindly gnome
of fear perched on my dashboard once, but we had all been instructed
to ignore the conditions of the chase. Here, it
seems to grow lighter with each passing century. No matter how you twist it,
life stays frozen in the headlights.
Funny, none of us heard the roar.

BALTIMORE

Two were alive. One came round the corner
clipclopping. Three were the saddest snow ever seen in Prairie City.

Take this, metamorphosis. And this. And this. And this.
If I'd needed your company,
I'd have curled up long before in the clock of weeds,
with only a skywriter to read by.
I'd have laved the preface
to the World's Collected Anthologies,
licked the henbane-flavored lozenge
and more. I'm presuming,
I know. And there are wide floodplains spotted with children,
investing everything in everything.
And I'm too shy to throw away.

COUSIN SARAH'S KNITTING

You keep asking me that four times.
Why trust me I think.
There is, in fact, nobody here.

Nobody in the past.
Nobody to turn to for advice.
A yellow flagpole rears thoughtfully.
Now if you were that nice.

He was pulled from space,
as from a shark. After they examined him
they let him go. What does that prove?

And called him Old Hickory.
As in hickory. No there were
at that time none living

out of a sideshow at the edge of a forest
and were mistreated in proportion,
with understanding, so they all grew

into the shade and for once it seemed
about right. Oh, call down to me.
It seemed about right.

Then there was something of a letdown.
Patrol boats converged
but it was decided that the . . .

and could continue its voyage
upriver
to the point where it tails off
        [. . .]

and then there was a large misunderstanding.
It was misunderstanding, mudsliding
from the side where the thing was let in.

And it was all goose, let me tell you,
braised goose. From which a longing in the original
loins came forward to mark you.

So many brave skippers,
such a long time at sea. But I was going
to remind you of this new story

I can't remember, of the two chums meeting in the overfed waste land and it supported
    them. And one got
off at the front. The other wandered for days and daze, and by the time nobody
    remembered it it was summer again
and wandered around defensively. Sure the organ meat
was pumping and somebody's boy came up to the correct
thing at the well head. Sure as you can claim Dixie your tax accountant
wandered over the remaining riviera, all to be blue again. And the rascals . . .
and I was going to say keep it. You can keep it.
Granted she has no reputation, an eye
here, another clovered savior here, they pretend to us, and it was time for the firemobile
    too.

LAST NIGHT I DREAMED I WAS IN BUCHAREST

seeking to convince the supreme Jester
that I am indeed the man in those commercials.
Simultaneously it peaked in Bolivia, the moon,
I mean. Then we were walking over what seemed to be
heather, or was called that. The downtown riot
of free speech occurred. Plastered to its muzzle,
Randy the dog's decoding apparatus went astray.
By then it was afternoon in much of the world;
iced tea was served on vast terraces
overlooking a crumbling sea. You can't juggle
four toddlers. Three is enough. Out of the beckoning
sea they arrived, in white ruffles with black coin-dots
attached; the lawn was closer to a farm
this time; it mouthed "Farm." Will vacuumed the whole of space
as far as the mind-your-own-business wire stretched, that is,
from Cadiz to Enterprise, Alaska. We thought we had seen a few new
adjectives, but nobody was too sure. They might have been
gerunds, or bunches of breakfast . . .

ADDED POIGNANCY

What could I tell you? I couldn't tell you any other way.
We, meanwhile, have witnessed changes, and now change
floods in from every angle. Stop me if you've heard this one,
but if you haven't, just go about your business. I'll catch up with you
at the exit. Who are the Blands? The second change was perhaps nothing more than
the possibility of changes, one by one, side by side, until the whole
canyon was carpeted with them. Nice. Summer, it said,
ever rested my mind. Something occurs everywhere then,
an immediate engagement with the atmosphere
we'd like to have around, but it was big, then, and obvious,
and oh, this is for your pains. No, really. Take it. I insist.

He thought if he lived amid leaves
everything would surface again, by which he meant, balance out,
only look what this random memory's done to him!
He eats no more, neither does he sleep. A permanent bell tone
seems to create his hearing at each moment of his elevator. Obey. We're
in for it. There are no two ways about it. Wait—
did I say two ways? That's it! *We'll fix his wagon with* too many *ways—*
so it'll be lopsided, with no judges to pay, and we can all go home.
Sweetheart? I fancy you now—

Hence it ends up with a scenario of them all getting paid,
the bums, and walking out into the eternal twilight
with gurus and girlfriends on their arms, one for each fist.
I like that way about it. I'm making believe
it never happened, that we got this way
merely by having been here forever. Millions of languages
became extinct, and not because there was nothing left to say in them,
but because it was all said too well, with
nary a dewdrop on the moment of glottal expulsion.
But now I've got to go put out the signs on the chairs

so folks'll know when to stop, and where, really, only a poodle
separates us from this life and the next.
It will take us longer to get from here to there.
And the cigar band is ecstatic,
stunning in its mauve and gold obsolescence,
an erratic bloom on sheer night, faintly deleterious . . .

LAUGHING GRAVY

The crisis has just passed.
Uh-oh, here it comes again,
looking for someone to blame itself on, you, I . . .

All these people coming in . . .
The last time we necked
I noticed this lobe on your ear.
Please, tell me we may begin.

All the wolves in the wolf factory paused
at noon, for a moment of silence.

FROM SUCH COMMOTION

The dress code is casual, the atmosphere relaxed
in the licensed quarters of our city;
young couples graciously stopping beneath umbrellas
in the street . . .

And this is not a thing that matters:
walks on grass, through flaring Adirondack chairs.
You caught me napping said the belle-lettriste.

No, perhaps it's not that, that's the point. You've
been in to see these?
And we should have decided to go there, gone for a second time.
Yes, well, they're working on it, et cetera, etc.

The summer capital exits past us, we have to
sell product. It "fell through" the European system,
now it's time for avatars. At four in the morning
the art demonstrations begin, psalteries jingle, the whole damn ocean
is there, up for review, for us. It's just

that we don't understand. It's my negative capability acting up
again. Well, I'm within my rights.
It's like apples and pears, or oranges and lemons,
what I always say.

From nests as admirable as these, wallpaper islands,
the vivid flow reverses. That's in-house.
And we go as far
With them as possible, suffer stupid reverses, get plastered,

    [. . .]

the goateed scorpion insists.
And it was while waiting for the drying to happen that we all got lost.
Please, he insisted, there's more to the point than two doors, O I know
it I said, I can't be damned to travel

any time. You should have pointed the way to me while I can,
while it's still light, otherwise what will all your gnashing accomplish,
the oatmeal? Please. Now just go away. It's
raining, the sun is shining, braver outdoors. Can we come listen to that.

Roll up your sleeves,
                              another day has ended. I am not a part of the vine
that was going to put me through school
but instead got sidetracked and wandered over the brink of an abyss
while we were having a good time
in full view of the nearest mountains. *Mon trésor,* she said, this is where I
disappear for a few moments, I want you to be brave.
Sure, nothing like a date in bed,
waking after midnight to the blank TV screen
that wants us all to listen to its cute life and someday understand
what rhomboids the earth took
on its way down to get us,
that we must be happy and sad forever after. No I don't think
it was in your best interests nor do I shave with an old-fashioned straight-edge,
you dolt. But I was coming to that,
doing the mystifying. So if he says not to be aloha, not again,
well gee in this old-fashioned bar, however will the runts learn from their again imploded
hair balls how straight everything is.

The rest, as they say, as they say, is history:
I captured a barracuda, it was midnight in the old steeple, the clans casually
moved on us, leggings barely jerked out of the ditch. It was folly
to be noticed, then, astir on the perhaps more urgent
surface of what becomes one, indeed comes to become one
through impossible rain and the sly glee of mirrored xylophones.
Say only it was one for the books,
and we, we did belong, though not to anything anybody'd recognize
as civil, or even territory. I need to subscribe,
now, history will carry me along and as gently leave me
here, in the cave, the enormous well-being
of which we may not speak.

THE BURDEN OF THE PARK

Each is truly a unique piece,
you said, or, perhaps, each
is a truly unique piece.
I sniff the difference.
It's like dust in an old house,
or the water thereof. Then you come
to an exciting part.
The bandit affianced
to the blind man's daughter. The mangel-wurzels
that come out of every door, salute the traveler
and are gone. Or the more melting pace of strolling players,
each with a collapsed sweetie on his arm, each
tidy as one's idea of everything under the sun is tidy.
And the wolverines
return, with their coach, and night,
the black bat night, is blacker than any bat.

Just so you know, this is the falling-off place,
for the water, where damsels stroll and uncles
know a good thing when they see one.
The park is all over.
It isn't a knee injury, or a postage stamp on Mars.
It is all of the above, and some other things too:
a nameless morning in May fielded by taut observers.
An inner tube on a couch.

Then we floated down the Great Array river, each
in our inner tube, each one a different color:
Mine was lime green, yours was pistachio.
And the current murmured to us mind your back
for another day. Are
you so sure we haven't passed the goalposts yet? Won't

you reconsider? Remount me to my source? Egad,
Trixie, the water can speak! Like a boy
it speaks, and I'm not so sure how little all this is,
how much fuss shouldn't be made about it. When another boy comes
to the edge of the falls, and calls, for it is late,
won't we be sorry for not having invented this one,
letting him fall by the wayside? Then, sure enough, waves
of heather recuse the bearers of false witness, they fly like ribbons
on the stiff breeze, telling of us: We once made
some mistake, it seems, and now we are to be judged, except
it isn't so bad, someone tells me you'll be let off the hook,
we will all be able to go home, sojourn and smile again, be racked
with insidious giggles like guilt. Meantime, jugglers swarm over the volcano's
stiff sides. We believe it to be Land's End, that it's
six o'clock, and the razor fish have gone home.

Once, on Mannahatta's bleak shore,
I trolled for spunkfish, but caught naught, nothing save
a rubber plunger or two. It was awful,
at that time. Now everything is cheerful.
I wonder, does it make a difference?
Are sailors waving
from the deck of their distraught ship? We aren't
envious though, life being so full of
so many little commotions, it's up to
whoever to grab his (or hers). The violin slices life up
into manageable hunks, and the fiddler knows not
who he is moving, or cares why people should be moved;
his mind is on the end, the extraordinary onus of finishing
what's set out for him. Do you imagine him better off than you?
My feet were numb, I ask him only, how do you carry this from here to over there?
Is there a flat barge? How many feet does a centipede have?

(Answer in tomorrow's edition.) I heard the weeping cranes,
telling how time was running out. It was Belgian,
they thought. Nobody burns the midnight oil for *this*,
yet I think I shall be a scholar someday, all the same.
The hours suit me. And the rubber corsages the girls wear
in and out of class. Sure, I'll turn out to be a nerd, and have to sit
in the corner, but that's part of the exciting adventure. I know things
are different and the same. Now if only I could tell you . . .

The period of my rest is ended.
I shall negotiate the fall, then go crying
back to you all. In those years peace came and went, our father's car changed
with the seasons, all around us was fighting and the excitement of spring.
Now, funnily enough, it's over. I shan't mind the vacant premise
that vexed me once. I know it's all too true. And the hooligan
ogles a calla lily: Maybe only the fingertips are exciting,
it thinks, disposing of another bushelful of ripe nostalgia.
Maybe it's too late,
maybe they came today.

DEAR SIR OR MADAM

After only a week of taking your pills
I confess I am seized with a boundless energy:
My plate fills up even as I scarf vegetable fragments
from the lucent blue around us. My firmament,

as I see it, was never this impartial.
The body's discomfiture, bodies of moonlit beggars,
sex in all its strangeness: Everything conspires
to hide the mess of inner living, raze
the skyscraper of inching desire.

Kill the grandchildren, leave a trail
of paper over the long interesting paths in the wood.
Transgress. In a word, be other than yourself
in turning into your love-soaked opposite. Plant
his parterre with antlers, burping
statue of when-was-the-last-time-you-saw Eros;

go get a job in the monument industry.

DISCORDANT DATA

for Mark Ford

Still in spring, my coat
travels with the pack, unbuttoned as they.

The weather report is useless. So,
sigh and begin again the letter.

"This is the first time in weeks
I've had to communicate with you. It all

falls, in balls of fire. I guess the
North Dakota landscape doesn't do much for you. Have you

no conscience, or conscious, conscious conscience?
May I remind you that every sentence, everywhere,

ends with a period? A disclaimer of sorts?"
He thought we'd gotten to the middle of the grass.

His glass fire hydrants can have no end.
Oh it was just an idea;

there, don't rail. The posse is coming
by for drinks, we can skip enslavement today.

Concentrate, instead, on this day's canonicity.
It has to be from somewhere,

right? Many prisoners have left downtown, the old man
assents. He was tremendous and bald. Liked a practical joke

[. . .]

now and again. Look, the white rain is writing on the wall
of his saloon. Could be he was over the hill,

we'd assumed, but the flapping in the net's too
strong for that. Don't you agree? Have you

had any further ideas on the subject? Yes, you
could well afford to give up a few.

Outside my window the Japanese driving range
shivers in its mesh veils, skinny bride
of soon-to-be-spring, ravenous, rapturous. Why is it here?
A puzzle. And what was it doing before, then? An earlier
puzzle. I like how it wraps itself
in not-quite wind—
                              sure enough,
the time is up. What else do you have in your hand?
Open your hand, please. My elder seraph
just woke up, is banging the coffee-pot lid
into place. See! the coffee flows
crazily to its nest, the doldrums are awake,
jumping up and down on tiptoe, night-blindness ended.

And from where *you* stand,
how many possible equations does it spell out?

My hair's just snoring back.
The coprophagic earth yields another of its
minute reasons, turns to a quivering mush,
recovers, staggers to its feet, touches the sky
with its yardstick, walks back to the place of received,
enthusiastic entities. Another year . . . And if we had known last spring
what the buildings knew then, what defeat, it would have turned to mud
all the same in us, waved us down the escalator,
past the counter with free samples of fudge, to where the hostess stands.
This was never my idea, shards, she says. This
is where the anonymous donors carved their initials in my book,
to be a puzzle for jaycees to come, as a nesting-ground
is to an island. Oh, we'd waddle
often, there, stepping in and out of the boat
as though nobody knew what time it was, or cared

which lid the horizon was. We'd get to know
each other in time, and till then it was all a camp meeting, hail-
fellow-well-met, and the barstools
reflected the ceiling's gummy polish, to the starboard
where purple kings sit, and it was too late for today,
the newspapers had already been printed, telling their tale
along avenues, husks of driftwood
washed ashore again and again, speechless, spun out of control.
What a gorgeous sunset, cigarette case, how tellingly
the coiled rope is modelled, what perfume
in that sound of thunder, invisible! And you wonder
why I came back? Perhaps *this* will refresh your memory,
skateboard, roller skates, the binomial theorem picked out in
brutish, swabbed gasps. All the way to the escape clause
he kept insisting he'd done nothing wrong, and then—pouf!—it was
curtains for him and us, excepting these splinters
of our perpetual remainder, reminder
of all those days to come, and those others, so far back
in the mothering past.

PROBABLY BASED ON A DREAM

Like you've done it before—
Are you working hard? Hello? Mrs. Grizzli?
             Only the happy few know what keeps us
from ballooning into our strength. And when we try
             to capture wisps from the rocket,
sinking in the hay, there are those who tell you
             to come again another day,
that the past is soiled and forgotten. Yet neither
             you nor I know what happens in the thud
of cannon threatening to take off with the wild ducks
             thunderously, and you, if I'm not
mistaken, were around here once, once too often
             the landlady tells me. Quick! Where is
your whoop? How unexpectedly have we arrived? In a brusque mountain
             workshop where tankas are forged, and the truth comes
unsliced, like bread, the captains and the pageants err and repeat;
             for nothing all along was it?
But someday, I know, my idol will slip me a pill
             for as long as bunkers repeat themselves. Alyssa?

Shovel the maps into the diving helmet.
The press cuttings have come to grief;
wind slaps the high buildings.
You too know Kokomo, O unpreceded one.

PROXIMITY

It was great to see you the other day
at the carnival. My enchiladas were delicious,

and I hope that yours were too.
I wanted to fulfill your dream of me

in some suitable way. Giving away my new gloves,
for instance, or putting a box around all that's wrong with us.

But these gutta-percha lamps do not whisper on our behalf.
Now sometimes in the evenings, I am lonely

with dread. A rambunctious wind fills the pine
at my doorstep, the woodbine is enchanted,

and I must be off before the clock strikes
whatever hour it is intent on.

Do not leave me in this wilderness!
Or, if you do, pay me to stay behind.

LIKE AMERICA

People are buying store-dolls.
I wonder if that's forbidden too.
Does it mean one isn't to lead one's life?

Today, a day that makes very little sense,
like America,
in clear disarray
everything's getting worse.
Besides, who are we not to endorse it?

And these shattered ornaments to truth
almost grew up to me.
The sun and the yard
paused over a thousand times,
unable to explain the arch that is daylight.

And the tribes that were before
this panicked band announced it was quitting
saw the crocuses too. They were purple and awful.

It's almost leaking to say it.
But how much longer could I go on not missing the point?

SNOW

As a fish spoils
in a time of truce, so these galoshes go
hopping over sidewalk and snowbank, not really knowing
to whose destiny we are being summoned
or what happens after that.

As time spoils,
it may have known what it was doing
but decided not to do anything about it, so everything is lost,
wrapped in a landfill. It could be caviar
or the New York *Daily News*.

After all, *I* come next,
he said, am a cruel object like all the torsos
you unbuttoned all over your previous life, scant in comparison
to this one, and I said, go ahead and quit clowning
if you like that game, but

leave me beside myself,
like a kid next to a lamppost. Okay, what gain
in not replying? What capitalist system do you think this is? Surely
it's late capitalism, by which I mean not to go
yet and peace undermines

the uproar we all made
about it, and you are positively put on hold
again. I like the mouse in this turmoil, not exactly purring
adroitly, not seeming to conjugate the
avalanche of fear.

     [. . .]

Now when Norsemen
(or some substitute) tumble out of the north, sifting
down over our busy, shuttered, dignified street with hints of the Azores,
there's no untangling the knots we put there before
and paused to identify

as the four winds rushed
in and purified the place of partnerships,
fanning overhead, a-bristle with doodads, chafing at every chime
from every earnest steeple, coughing too much.
The little guy was

impatient, was serious,
every time a blow fell adjured another conspirator,
and so, when it got quite dark we became an outing, another
quilting-bee disaster. And if it tried too far
there was always salt to rub

in wounds to be licked.

THE DONG WITH THE LUMINOUS NOSE

(a cento)

Within a windowed niche of that high hall
I wake and feel the fell of dark, not day.
I shall rush out as I am, and walk the street
hard by yon wood, now smiling as in scorn.
The lights begin to twinkle from the rocks
from camp to camp, through the foul womb of night.
Come, Shepherd, and again renew the quest.
And birds sit brooding in the snow.

Continuous as the stars that shine,
when all men were asleep the snow came flying
near where the dirty Thames does flow
through caverns measureless to man,
where thou shalt see the red-gilled fishes leap
and a lovely Monkey with lollipop paws
where the remote Bermudas ride.

Softly, in the dusk, a woman is singing to me:
This is the cock that crowed in the morn.
Who'll be the parson?
Beppo! That beard of yours becomes you not!
A gentle answer did the old Man make:
Farewell, ungrateful traitor,
bright as a seedsman's packet
where the quiet-coloured end of evening smiles.

Obscurest night involved the sky
and brickdust Moll had screamed through half a street:
"Look in my face; my name is Might-have-been,
sylvan historian, who canst thus express
every night and alle

the happy highways where I went
to the hills of Chankly Bore!"

Where are you going to, my pretty maid?
These lovers fled away into the storm
and it's O dear, what can the matter be?
For the wind is in the palm-trees, and the temple bells they say:
Lay your sleeping head, my love,
on the wide level of a mountain's head,
thoughtless as monarch oaks, that shade the plain,
in autumn, on the skirts of Bagley Wood.
A ship is floating in the harbour now,
heavy as frost, and deep almost as life!

COME ON, DEAR

It was another era, almost another century,
I was going to say. The saint wept quietly
in her ebony pew. It was the thing to do.
Then garlands of laughter, studded with cloves and lemons,
joined the standing figures with their distant nimbi.
Inexplicably, all was well for a time.

Soon, discordant echoes reined in the heyday:
It was love, after all,
that everybody was talking about
and nobody gave a shit for.
But why am I telling *you* about all this, who wrote the book,
who stamped his initials in the fairway
for all blokes to see? And if it only came
down to this smidgen, would apes and penguins be any wiser
for all the tunnels of love we shuffled through,
scared by skeletons, by bats, at every turning
of our loose-leafed trajectory through shallow water?

Only, when the iodine sunset
bleeds again against red day, will all children
get permission to go out where the grass is short,
where the absent-minded postman leaves earnests of his passing
from this day to the next, where the eaves are clipped
close to the houses. Five days from the last clerestory
your ambiance drained into the pockmarked shutters.
Obviously the jig was up. What's that? Whose jig? O I can see clear
ahead into the flying; the poor don't talk much about it,
but her apron is ambrosial with trellised stars,
her stance stares down even the most unquiet,
and on days like this you ride free.

There was such numismatics in his pocket
as only jitterbugs in cyberspace could conjugate
while from fate's awning the diamond drip descended, bigger
than both of us, big as all outdoors.

HOMECOMING

Weather drips quietly through the skeins
in my diary. What surly elision is this?

Who faxed the folks news of my homecoming,
even unto the platform number? The majestic parlor car
slides neatly into its berth, the doors fly open,
and it's Jean and Marcy and all the kids, waving pink plastic pinwheels,
chomping on popcorn. Ngarrrh. You know I adore ceremony,
even while refusing to stand on it, but this, this is too inane.
And the cold anonymity of the station takes over,
reins in the crowds that were sifting to the farthest exits. No one is here.
Now I know why I've always hated the tango, yet loved the intimacy
secreted in its curls. And for this to continue, we've got to
get together, renew old saws, let old grudges ride . . .

Later I'm posting this to you.
I just thought of you, you see, as indeed I do
several million times a day. I need your disapproval,
can't live without your churlish ways.

from GIRLS ON THE RUN

[sections I, II, III, VIII, IX, XXI of XXI]

(1999)

GIRLS ON THE RUN

after Henry Darger

I.

A great plane flew across the sun,
and the girls ran along the ground.
The sun shone on Mr. McPlaster's face, it was green like an elephant's.

Let's get out of here, Judy said.
They're getting closer, I can't stand it.
But you know, our fashions are in fashion
only briefly, then they go out
and stay that way for a long time. Then they come back in
for a while. Then, in maybe a million years, they go out of fashion
and stay there.
Laure and Tidbit agreed,
with the proviso that after that everyone would become fashion
again for a few hours. Write it now, Tidbit said,
before they get back. And, quivering, I took the pen.

Drink the beautiful tea
before you slop sewage over the horizon, the Principal directed.
OK, it's calm now, but it wasn't two minutes ago. What do you want me to do, said Henry,
I am no longer your serf,
and if I was I wouldn't do your bidding. That is enough, sir.
You think you can lord it over every last dish of oatmeal
on this planet, Henry said. But wait till my ambition
comes a cropper, whatever that means, or bursts into feathered bloom
and burns on the shore. Then the kiddies dancing sidewise
declared it a treat, and the ice-cream gnomes slurped their last that day.

Inside, in the twilit nest of evening,
something was coming undone. Dimples could feel it,
surging over her shoulder like a wave of energy. And then—

it was gone. No one had witnessed it but herself.
And so Dimples took off for the city, which was near and wholesome.
There, with her sister Larissa, she planned the big blue boat
that future generations will live in, and thank us for. It twitched
at its steely moorings, and seemed to say: Live, like life, with me.

Let the birds wash over them, Laure said, for what use are earmuffs
in a snowstorm, except to call attention to distant tots
who have strayed. And now the big Mother warms them,
accepts them, for the nervous predicates they are. Far from the beach-fiend's
howling, their adventure nurses itself back
to something like health. On the fifth day it takes a little blancmange
and stands up, only to fall back into a hammock.
I told you it was coming, cried Dimples, but look out,
another big one is on the way!
And they all ran, and got out, and that was that for that day.

    II.
Hungeringly, Tidbit approached the crone who held the bowl,
. . . drank the honey. It had good things about it.
Now, pretty as a moment,
Tidbit's housecoat sniffed the undecipherable,
the knowable past. They were anxious
to get back to work. Diane was looking relaxed.
Then, some say, Pete said
it was the afternoon backing up again, inexorable
with dreams, looking for garbage to pick a fight with.
"My goodness! Do you suppose his blowhole's . . . ?"

Sometime later they returned with Pete and the others,
he all excited, certain he had spotted a fuse this time.

Rags the mutt licked and yelped. "Oh, get down!"
But Rags seemed to be on to something. "And if they come
through the alfalfa this time, we'll have a nice idea
of where they are, of who these men are. If they abrade
the abandoned silo, no one will be wiser. Look, their pastel
tent, and flags made from the same substance, waving *dehors*—
I've got to get an angle on this, a firm tack of some kind."
Willingly, the flood washed over the day
and so much that was complicated, from the past:
the tiny doggy door Rags had made with a T-square,
surplus sequins.
        And if they don't want to play
according to our rules, what then? "Why, then
we'll come up with something, like the sink-drain.
Anyway, this is all just an excuse for you to leave your posts,
toying with anagrams, while the real message
is being written in the stars. To go ahead,
it says, but be watchful for scouts
in the corn shocks. This close to Halloween there are lots of little bumps
around, and tea cosies to shroud them. Beware one last time;
but as the spirit of going is to go, I can't
control you, advise you much longer. Just keep on
persevering, and then we'll know what we have done matters most to us."
With that, the sticks uprooted the tent.
A thousand passions came unleashed,
but fortunately for the girls, none of them were around to witness it—
they were off in a cage with the canaries.
        Now, though,
when it came time to vote for who the deed was done
by, the others mattered too. It was just their pot luck.

    [. . .]

Oh well, Laure offered, we were going to close down that shaftway
anyway, and the subway came close: It was Mother and her veering
playthings again, torn between the impossible alternatives of existing
and saying no to menace. To everyone's surprise the bus stopped.
Our stalwart little band of angels got on it, and were taken for a ride
into the next chapter, a dim place of curlicues and bas-reliefs.
If I had a handle, Laure thought.

III.

Out in Michigan, or was it Minnesota, though, time had stopped
to see what it could see, which wasn't much. A recent hooligan scare had blighted the
   landscape,
lowering the temperature by several degrees. "Having
to pee ruins my crinoline relentlessly,
because it comes only ecstatically."
But the wounded cow knew otherwise.

                                        She was at least sixty,
had many skins covering her own, regal one. So then they all cry,
at sea. The lawnmower is emitting sparks again,
one doesn't know how many, or how much faster it will have to go
to meet us at the Denizens' by six o'clock. We'd have been better
off letting the prisoners stage their own war. Now I don't know
so much, and with Aunt Jennie at my side we could release
a few more bombs and not know it.

                                Everywhere in the tangled schist
someone was living, it seemed to say, this is my doing;
whoever shall come afterward is a delusion. And I went round
the corner to say, Well it sure looks like an improvement—hey,
why don't you tie your shoes, and then your bonnet will be picture-perfect?

      [. . .]

No, only getting away
has any value to her: A stone's throw is better than a mile
since one will have to be up again much later, and this way
saves time. How often did you let your mother say,
How did you get your Sundays packed away? And yet it's always treasonable
to be in the middle. H'm, there are objections to that,
just as I thought. This might help. Yes. But the color
of this paint is too fabulous, I'd asked for something fragmented
like sea-spray. In that case we cannot be of service to you. Farewell.

Now I had walked the terrible byways for what seemed like too long.
Now another was following, insensately.
Would there be foodstuffs on the steps? How did that ladder point into nowhere?
"Shuffle, you miser!" Just so, Shuffle said,
I don't want to be around when the gang erupts
into centuries of inviolate privilege, and cisterns tumble down
the side of the slope, and all is gone more or less naturally to hell.
To which Dimples replied, Why not? Why not just give yourself, one time,
to the floods of human resources that are our day?
Because I don't want to live at an angle to the blokes who micromanage
our territory, that's all. Oh, who do you mean? Why, the red-trimmed zebras,
Shuffle said, that people thinks is the cutest damn things in town
until the victory bonfire on the square, and then there's more racing
and chasing than you can shake a banjo-string at,
and it'll have muddled you over by the time the war has crested.

He sat, eating a cheese sandwich, wondering if it would be his last,
fiddled and sank away.
                                        And as far as the wires
could stretch, into the inevitable jerk-kingdom, the little girl
crawled on her hands and feet. That was no jack-in-the-box
back there, that was the real thing.
     [. . .]

Yes, Stuart Hofnagel, they came to you, they'd expected big things
of you back in Arkadelphia, and now you were a soured loner like anybody.
Old town, you seem to remember otherwise.
That was you backing into love, wasn't it? So we all came and were glad that day.
That was all a fine day for us. Happiness, that we loved you so much;
phony energy, because we were happy.
Yet the town held back, rinsing her skirts
in the dour brook that fled the sawmill, just before four o'clock.
None of us slaves knew any different, having been nursed into solitude the night before
     last.
Certainly, if someone knocks on the open door
we will be pleasant, and look after the stranger just as if he were one of our own.
That's the way we were made. We can't help it. Conversely,
if a friend obtrudes his thinking into this plan of ours,
we shall deny all knowledge of him. It happens this way in the wilderness.
Plus the pot is full of old oddments. The rhubarb stains on Peggy's frock
almost—but not quite—match its rickrack trim.
That's where the human aspect comes in.
Some were born to play with, to think constantly about it, with a nod,
not much more, to the future and what its executives might have in store.
We aren't easily intimidated.
And yet we are always frightened,
frightened that this will come to pass
and we all unable to do anything about it, in case it ever does.
So we appeal to you, sun, on this broad day.
You were ever a helpmate in times of great churning, and fatigue.
You make us forget how serious we are
and we dance in the lightning of your rhythm like demented souls
on a hospital spree. If only,
when the horse crawls up your back, you had known to make more of it.
But the climate is military, and yet one can't see too far ahead.

Better a storehouse of pearls than this battered shoehorn
of wood, yet it can cause everything to take place and change for you.

VIII.
"All aboard! If there's one thing I hate it's a loner,"
Uncle Philip said, or someone who's beside himself. Please, Uncle,
can't we go out today? Aw, shut up, Philip said. Now there were two bald uncles
who lived in the nearby swamp. One of them knew Shuffle. And he said:
If it's to play in, why not. But if it's just to play over and around
then I don't see why you need to, and indeed shall expend every effort
to see that you don't. But if the mirror
refract any of this, then boy you can be sure you can go.
And in a little while the mirror reflected all of them
back at each other. This was exceptional. Those getting up to leave were stayed
in their rubber boots, and those arriving were perplexed and pleasured. Why, isn't
it a rebus, Aunt Clara wondered, and Tootles agreed that it was.
From a distant patch of loam the speck started arriving, bigger
with each hulking gasp. Why doesn't the foreman go, someone wondered, it's
part of his job description, and the others can go anyway, if they want to. So all
got to be sensitized. And in the large gap for brooding that was created
some of the saner heads got wind of the passing football
and were mortified into a decision. Sun shovel it in,
there's no more room for today, and you can go. I said you can go.
Oh, the man said, not understanding, and a third time they shouted at him:
You can go.
And he betook himself on his two legs.

Under frozen mounds of yak butter the graffiti have their day, and are elaborate,
some say. Nobody wants to go there. Yes, she said, we will swim
there if necessary. The arroz con pollo can take us

and do with us what we will. Just as I thought I had found a solution
to this and other present error, the knitting needles collapsed.
Never bathe or shave on a cloudy day, Uncle Margaret cautioned. The twins were in
    limbo
over this but we steered the car carefully, permanently
toward them and they too were saved. Hey,
we put it all aside for a rainy day, and this is one, and this is just superior,
Dave asserted. And all we've got to do is roll over
and the dream will be over. Not so fast, Aunt Clara indicated, the gum
trees are a-rattle. The stealth of the horizon
nears us. That cat is asleep. And who shall take the dinner pail out
to the sodden farmhands, and just leave? Be it us,
that will be all OK. And in two strokes it was done. And they came and cancelled
the signature, so that everything was as it had been before. The militia capsized
and died from eating a certain kind of mold. Now the sentry wanes,
sinks and dies of its own weight. All the marbles have rolled inside the house.

    IX.
And now everyone must sleep.
The kiddies are silent for a while,

and yes, singly or in pairs,
they come down to the water's edge, to drink their fill. The wide-eyed pansies gaze
immutably. Rev up the old flivver, we'll be disparate for a time
and then we'll see, the mice will see. Why all the fuss?
You know you came here just for this, this kiss, on the face, the dog said.
Where are you starting to go? Are my pants too wide?
What if someone else on the other side of the globe
told you this, would he fall off? Would I?
That's why they say stand clear.
You can never do yourself favors enough, in the rosebush

from which man never extricates himself. I see,
someone said. Does it matter about being alone? No it's important
but not that important. I see, this person said. But then what if I am
no longer alone? What then? Two of you can board as long as one stays on the lookout,
the relaxed policeman said. He brought a sandwich down the street
and placed it on the curb, he was so nice. We didn't expect the birches
to explode just then. The sound traveled over the neighboring hills
down to the makeshift waterfront, lugubrious in the darkening air.
It's the cold
again he said. Every time I forget something, whenever anything is in motion
again, this happens, and I am not prepared for it. I'm plum scared.
Then you should go out,
your dress will be as morning to the cows,
she said. And he did and it was.

By and by Allen told us of a scheme
to rescue Pliable, if the latter consented, which surely he would,
and it would all seem as if it had never been.
But it would have, we'd know that, and ever after, as adults,
wandering the velveteen streets, we'd come upon someone who would have known
      someone
who wasn't all there and we'd be back at square one in the love market
and oceans of tremors would have been discovered. A word
would issue from a crack in the pavement, and it was up to Jane and the detective to
      decide
whether they'd heard it. If they hadn't, fine.
Otherwise it's down to the station
to sort everything out in the middle of the night, and not taken to too kindly
either. Drunks passed back and forth. Jane
was titillated but squeamish. She thought of asking Cupid
if the seams of her stockings were straight, but Pliable intervened strenuously,
arguing that no two people can take love into their own hands.

Oh. Excuse me. Bye bye. I'm
outta here. No, said Jane, you don't
understand, he means to be nice. He's a sheep, really. Yes but I don't see
how that affects me, and anyway I'm not interested. Oh, please, you must be,

she agitated, just for a little while as we perch
on this twig that must be the end of the world for us. Jolly good,
Pliable thought, it's me or you, now or never and here comes—

I awoke from the dream. A big boom
was passing over my head. I could see clear up the mizzen, if that counts,
anymore, your honor, I just want to say I respects
all what is good, and don't come here any more, I won't. That is good.
We'll take off and be back pronto. Don't
answer the telephone until dawn. Supposing they come and
want to ask you and we are gone, or in the middle of something? That's OK but don't
be gone too long. We'll come too.

I'm no expert but I see a problem here.
The fisheries have come undone, as the headlong race to the pole
has made alarmingly evident. As I say, I can speak only for myself,
but as soon as I got here the rules became different.
They didn't apply to me anymore, or to anyone else except a distant runt,
almost invisible in its litter. So how was
I to know who to stand up to, when to turn abrasive, when all things nestled,
equidistant, all hearts were charming, and it was good to be natural and sincere?
True, we had much to worry about,
other things to think about, but when has mankind had the leisure
to distract himself from these and other unassailable syllogisms?
So the truth just washed up on the shore,
a bundle of nerves, not resembling much of anything
we cared to remember. Was polite, stoical,

and anything else to deflect attention from its seething ambiguity.
It was time to come back, back into the flower-bedecked house.
A stunning moment of certainty survived
briefly, then it too was washed away in the rising flood,
tortured, unambitious.
School was over,
not just for that day but forever and for seasons to come.
The reason was that the truth was just average
on the iniquity scale, and nobody wanted to get involved.

XXI.

When more and more people come to you, you know
what they are saying, and you know how to deal with them.
Many were the whiskers that applied that day,
and many the salvage operations bent on rejecting them.
If you have some ointment it would be good to use it
now. Otherwise the opportunity may never again present itself.
I know you mean well, Hopeful murmured. Talkative was
starting to tell one of his stories again, and smiling,
Hopeful silently abetted it. He knew the old boy was feeling his oats,
which was fine with him, as he too was feeling good. Talkative, you old so-
and-so, he volunteered. Then his father-in-law blew up. The Overall Boys, fishing poles
    in hand,
charged into nether regions.
Susie never thought she'd see the day when so much surplus was at stake,
and she alone, outdoors, waiting for the postman's red bicycle
for what seemed like ages. He explained that it was a routine assassination,
that that was what had delayed him. Crestfallen, Susie hardly dared look up
into the eyes of her man, a breeze was blowing, it was snowing. The droplets made
    diagonal streaks in the air
where pterodactyls had been. It was time for an exodus of sorts;

Paul picked up the legend
                    where it had been broken off: "No
blame accrues to those who were left behind, unless, haply, they were climbing
the wall to get a better view of the stars, in which case the next-to-last
must pay a tribute, and so on. It can be anything, old money,
a calico scarf, whatever has soiled the hand of the donor by staying
to wear out its welcome. O in time it will shrivel.
What is it to imagine something you had forgotten once, is it
inventing, or more of a restoration from ancient mounds that were probably there?
You that can tell all, tell this."

At first Talkative was reluctant to speak, then the words fell
like spring rain from his lips, all was as it had been before,
with no two dancers in step, and a bright, really bright light exploded
above the barn. A horse wanders away
and is abruptly inducted into the carousel,
eyes flying, mane askew. There is no end to the dance,
even death pales in comparison, and at the same time we are forced to
take into account the likelihood of the moment's behaving badly, the eventual cost
to our side in terms of dignity, compromised integrity. Twelve princesses
stepped ashore, no one knew them, they too seemed not to know where they were.
"In what region . . ." one began timidly, then the whole flock took off
like a shout, leaving the beleaguered ground to fend for itself.
"There were picture books at that time,
and dreams woven in and out of them. But one was not to notice,
only to go on behaving. And at the end, when everything was added up,
we probably owed them a penny. It's enough to make you weep.
But skies are gilded and armored, we shall put a brave face

on it for a time, then school will be over, and sublime rest
flow from the uncorked flask like a prodigious perfume,
or sleep, a potent but dangerous brew,

a new assignment. Then we can get out of hock,
redeem Daddy's dear old coupons." He broke off, not wanting to bestir
the others, who had in fact ceased to hear, so monotonous
was the noise of his voice, like rain that flails the spears of vetch
in Maytime, to reap a tiny investment.
So we faced the new day,
like a pilgrim who sees the end of his journey deferred forever.
Who could predict where we would be led, to what
extremes of aloneness? Yet the horizon is civil.

A struggle ensued and the driver fell out of the vehicle.
And what did the old lady do then?
"She gave them some broth, without any bread, and . . . and . . ."

All are like soup.

So if it pleases you to come
out we all await thy pleasure, Stuart Hofnagel.
Who was with Young Topless? It seemed then an abyss was forming,
a new set of lagoons. More than look past it
one cannot, for more
than that is denied us.
So have I heard it said in old kingdoms, it said.
Larkspur towering over miniature turrets. The bandoleer was shot to hell.

The spa looked closed. So,
if you are in the market for a steeple, I commend this one
rigorously. It was not given to human divination to exhume it
like the comet, but to pause briefly, the blind
man's praise will cook itself. A giant paw
over the moon. Melons bloomed in corners. Shrimp blew away
to be fecund elsewhere, next year.

In time it will be your caesura too, but we mustn't
think of that. We caregivers especially. We must forget,
while others only live, peer into circles of living embroidery. The geese
will jump for you again, anon. Then it's no business. They closed
the place, the food court, they all
have gone away, it's restless, and mighty, as an ark
to the storm, yet the letter
of the law is obeyed, and sometimes the spirit
in forgotten tales of the seekers—O who were they?
Mary Ann, and Jimmy—no, but who were they?
Who have as their mantles on the snow
and we shall never reach land
before dark, yet who knows what advises them,
discreet in the mayhem? And then it's bright in the defining pallor of their day.
Does this clinch anything? We were cautioned once, told not to venture out—
yet I'd offer this much, this leaf, to thee.
Somewhere, darkness churns and answers are riveting,
taking on a fresh look, a twist. A carousel is burning.
The wide avenue smiles.

from YOUR NAME HERE

(2000)

THIS ROOM

The room I entered was a dream of this room.
Surely all those feet on the sofa were mine.
The oval portrait
of a dog was me at an early age.
Something shimmers, something is hushed up.

We had macaroni for lunch every day
except Sunday, when a small quail was induced
to be served to us. Why do I tell you these things?
You are not even here.

In town it was very urban but in the country cows were covering the hills. The clouds were near and very moist. I was walking along the pavement with Anna, enjoying the scattered scenery. Suddenly a sound like a deep bell came from behind us. We both turned to look. "It's the words you spoke in the past, coming back to haunt you," Anna explained. "They always do, you know."

Indeed I did. Many times this deep bell-like tone had intruded itself on my thoughts, scrambling them at first, then rearranging them in apple-pie order. "Two crows," the voice seemed to say, "were sitting on a sundial in the God-given sunlight. Then one flew away."

"Yes . . . *and then*?" I wanted to ask, but I kept silent. We turned into a courtyard and walked up several flights of stairs to the roof, where a party was in progress. "This is my friend Hans," Anna said by way of introduction. No one paid much attention and several guests moved away to the balustrade to admire the view of orchards and vineyards, approaching their autumn glory. One of the women however came to greet us in a friendly manner. I was wondering if this was a "harvest home," a phrase I had often heard but never understood.

"Welcome to my home . . . well, to our home," the woman said gaily. "As you can see, the grapes are being harvested." It seemed she could read my mind. "They say this year's vintage will be a mediocre one, but the sight is lovely, nonetheless. Don't you agree, Mr. . . ."

"Hans," I replied curtly. The prospect was indeed a lovely one, but I wanted to leave. Making some excuse I guided Anna by the elbow toward the stairs and we left.

"That wasn't polite of you," she said dryly.

"Honey, I've had enough of people who can read your mind. When I want it done I'll go to a mind reader."

"I happen to be one and I can tell you what you're thinking is false. Listen to what the big bell says: 'We are all strangers on our own turf, in our own time.' You should have paid attention. Now adjustments will have to be made."

It crossed the road so as to avoid having to greet me. "Poor thing but mine own," I said, "without a song the day would never end." Warily the thing approached. I pitied its stupidity so much that huge tears began to well up in my eyes, falling to the hard ground with a plop. "I don't need a welcome like that," it said. "I was ready for you. All the ladybugs and the buzzing flies and the alligators know about you and your tricks. Poor, cheap thing. Go away, and take your song with you."

Night had fallen without my realizing it. Several hours must have passed while I stood there, mulling the grass and possible replies to the hapless creature. A mason still stood at the top of a ladder repairing the tiles in a roof, by the light of the moon. But there was no moon. Yet I could see his armpits, hair gushing from them, and the tricks of the trade with which he was so bent on fixing that wall.

"Her name is Liz, and I need her in my biz," I hummed wantonly. A band of clouds all slanted in the same direction drifted across the hairline horizon like a tribe of adults and children, all hastening toward some unknown destination. A crisp pounding. Done to your mother what? Are now the . . . And so you understand it, she . . . I. Once you get past the moralizing a new winter twilight creeps into place. And a lot of guys just kind of live through it? Ossified soup, mortised sloop. Woody has the staff to do nothing. You never know what. That's what I think. Like two notes of music we slid apart, far from one another's protective jealousy. The old cat, sunning herself, had no problem with that. Nor did the diaphanous trains of fairies that sagged down from a sky that suggested they had never been anywhere, least of all there. At the time we had a good laugh over it. But it did hurt. It still does. That's what I think, he slapped.

Sometimes the drums would actually let us play
between beats, and that was nice. Before closing time.
By then the clown's anus
would get all chewed up by the donkey
that hated having a tail pinned on it,
which was perhaps understandable. The three-legged midgets
ran around, they enjoyed hearing us play so much,
and the saxophone had something to say
about all this, but only to itself.

Clusters of pollen blot out the magnolia blossoms this year
and that's about all there is to it. Like I said,
it's pretty much like last year, except for Brooke.
She was determined to get a job in the city. When last heard from
she had found one, playing a sonata of Beethoven's (one
of the easier ones) in the window of a department store
downtown somewhere, and then that closed, the whole city did,
tighter'n a drum. So we have only our trapezoidal reflections
to look at in its blue glass sides, and perhaps admire—
oh, why can't this be some other day? The children all came over
(we thought they were midgets at first) and wanted
to be told stories to, but mostly to be held.
John I think did the right thing by shoveling them under the carpet.

And then there were the loose wickets
after the storm, and that made croquet impossible.
Hailstones the size of medicine balls were rolling down the slope anyway
right toward our doorstep. Most of them melted before they got there, but one,
a particularly noxious one, actually got in the house and left its smell,
a smell of violets, in fact, all over the hall carpet,
which didn't cancel one's rage at breaking and entering,
of all crimes the most serious, don't you fear?
        [. . .]

I've got to finish this. Father will be after me.
Oh, and did the red rubber balls ever arrive? We could do something
with them, I just have to figure out what.
Today a stoat came to tea
and that was so nice it almost made me cry—
look, the tears in the mirror are still streaming down my face
as if there were no tomorrow. But there is one, I fear,
a nice big one. Well, so long,
and don't touch any breasts, at least until I get there.

You are my most favorite artist. Though I know
very little about your work. Some of your followers I know:
Mattia Preti, who toiled so hard to so little
effect (though it was enough). Luca Giordano, involved
with some of the darkest reds ever painted, and lucent greens,
thought he had discovered the secret of the foxgloves.
But it was too late. They had already disappeared
because they had been planted in some other place.
Someone sent some bread up
along with a flask of wine, to cheer him up,
but the old, old secret of the foxgloves, never
to be divined, won't ever go away.

I say, if you were toting hay up the side of a stack
of it, that might be Italian. Or then again, not.
We have these things in Iowa,
too, and in the untrained reaches of the eyelid
hung out, at evening, over next to nothing. What was it she had said,
back there, at the beginning? "The flowers
of the lady next door are beginning to take flight,
and what will poor Robin do then?" It's true, they were blasting off
every two seconds like missiles from a launching pad, and nobody wept, or even cared.
Look out of the window, sometime, though, and you'll see
where the difference has been made. The song of the shrubbery
can't drown out the mystery of what we are made of,
of how we go along, first interested by one thing and then another
until we come to a wide avenue whose median
is crowded with trees whose madly peeling bark is the color of a roan,
perhaps, or an Irish setter. One can wait on the curb for the rest
of one's life, for all anyone cares, or one can cross
when the light changes to green, as in the sapphire folds
of a shot-silk bodice Luca Giordano might have bothered with.

Now it's life. But, as Henny Penny said to Turkey Lurkey, something
is hovering over us, wanting to destroy us, but waiting,
though for what, nobody knows.

In the night of the museum, though, some whisper like stars
when the guards have gone home, talking freely to one another.
"Why did that man stare, and stare? All afternoon it seemed he stared
at me, though he obviously saw nothing. Only a fragment of a vision
of a lost love, next to a pool. I couldn't deal with it
much longer, but luckily I didn't have to. The experience
is ending. The time for standing to one side is near
now, very near."

INDUSTRIAL COLLAGE

We are constantly running checks.
Quantity control is our concern here, you see.
No batch is allowed to leave the premises
without at least a superficial glance along the tops
of the crates. For who knows how much magic
may be imprisoned there?

Likewise, when the product reaches the market
we like to kind of keep an eye on things there too.
Complaints about the magic
have dwindled to a mere trickle in recent years.
Still you never know if some guy's going to get funny
and tamper with the equation, causing
apocalyptic sighs to break out in the streets,
barking dogs, skidding vehicles, and the whole consignment
of ruthless consequences. That is why we keep a team of experts
on hand, always awake, alert for the slightest thread of disorder
on someone's pants. In spring these incidents can double, quadruple, even.
Everything wants to be let out of its box come April or May
and we have to test-drive the final result before it's been gummed
into the album dark farces regulate. Someone, then, must be constantly
on duty, as well as a relief contingent, for this starry mass
to continue revolving.

Like an apple on the ground
it looks at you. The neighborhood police were kind,
arrested a miscreant, though he was never brought to trial,
which is normal for this type of event.
Meanwhile spring edges inexorably into summer,
where, paradoxically, there is more activity but less to show for it.
The merry-go-rounds begin turning in the carnivals of August.

Best to leave prison till winter, once the honor system has broken down.
A stalemate could pollute new beginnings.
November tells it best, in a whisper almost,
so that there is surprisingly little letdown,
only this new background, a finer needle to thread.

THE HISTORY OF MY LIFE

Once upon a time there were two brothers.
Then there was only one: myself.

I grew up fast, before learning to drive,
even. There was I: a stinking adult.

I thought of developing interests
someone might take an interest in. No soap.

I became very weepy for what had seemed
like the pleasant early years. As I aged

increasingly, I also grew more charitable
with regard to my thoughts and ideas,

thinking them at least as good as the next man's.
Then a great devouring cloud

came and loitered on the horizon, drinking
it up, for what seemed like months or years.

Dewey took Manila
and soon after invented the decimal system
that keeps libraries from collapsing even unto this day.
A lot of mothers immediately started naming their male offspring "Dewey,"
which made him queasy. He was already having second thoughts about imperialism.
In his dreams he saw library books with milky numbers
on their spines floating in Manila Bay.
Soon even words like "vanilla" or "mantilla" would cause him to vomit.
The sight of a manila envelope precipitated him
into his study, where all day, with the blinds drawn,
he would press fingers against temples, muttering "What have I done?"
all the while. Then, gradually, he began feeling a bit better.
The world hadn't ended. He'd go for walks in his old neighborhood,
marveling at the changes there, or at the lack of them. "If one is
to go down in history, it is better to do so for two things
rather than one," he would stammer, none too meaningfully.

One day his wife took him aside
in her boudoir, pulling the black lace mantilla from her head
and across her bare breasts until his head was entangled in it.
"Honey, what am I supposed to say?" "Say nothing, you big boob.
Just be glad you got away with it and are famous." "Speaking of
boobs . . ." "Now you're getting the idea. Go file those books
on those shelves over there. Come back only when you're finished."

    [. . .]

To this day schoolchildren wonder about his latter career
as a happy pedant, always nice with children, thoughtful
toward their parents. He wore a gray ceramic suit
walking his dog, a "bouledogue," he would point out.
People would peer at him from behind shutters, watchfully,
hoping no new calamities would break out, or indeed
that nothing more would happen, ever, that history had ended.
Yet it hadn't, as the admiral himself
would have been the first to acknowledge.

HEARTACHE

Sometimes a dangerous slice-of-life
like stepping off a board-game
into a frantic lagoon

drags the truth from the bathroom, where it has been hiding.
"Do whatever you like to improve the situation,
and—good luck," it added, like a barber adding an extra plop of lather

to a stupefied customer's face. "When they let you out
I'll be waiting for you." It had been that way ever since a girl with braids
teased him about getting too short. Yeah, and I'll bet they have

places for people like you too. Trouble is, I don't know of any.
The years whirled quickly by, an upward spiral
toward what ghastly ascendency? He didn't know. He cried.

One November the police chief came calling.
He had secretly been collecting all the bright kids
in the universe, popping them into a big bag

which he lugged home with him. No one was too sure what happened
after that. The kids were past caring; they had the run
of the house after all. Was it so much better outside?

Snow lashed the windowpanes as though punishing them
for having the property of being seen through. The little town
grew quieter. No one missed the kids. They had been too bright

for that to happen. Night sprang out of the dense cold
like an infuriated ocelot with her cub that someone had been trying
to steal, or so it pretended. The frightened townspeople sped away.

[. . .]

There was no longer any room on the sidewalk
for anything but "v's" drawn in pink chalk, the way a child
draws a seagull. Down at the tavern the neon glowed a comforting

red. "All beer on tap," it said, and
"Booths for Ladies."

REDEEMED AREA

Do you know where you live? Probably.
Abner is getting too old to drive but won't admit it.
The other day he got in his car to go buy some cough drops
of a kind they don't make anymore. And the drugstore
has been incorporated into a mall about seven miles away
with only about half the stores rented. There are three
other malls within a four-mile area. All the houses
are owned by the same guy, who's been renting
them out to college students for years, so they are virtually uninhabitable.
A smell of vitriol and socks pervades the area
like an open sewer in a souk. Anyway the cough drops
(a new brand) tasted pretty good—like catnip
or an orange slice that has lain on a girl's behind.

That's the electrician calling now—
nobody else would call before 7 A.M. Now we'll have some
electricity in the place. I'll start by plugging in
the Christmas tree lights. They were what made the whole thing
go up in sparks the last time. Next, the light
by the dictionary stand, so I can look some words up.
Then probably the toaster. A nice slice

of toast would really hit the spot now. I'm afraid it's all over
between us, though. Make nice, like you really cared,
I'll change my chemise, and we can dance around the room
like demented dogs, eager for a handout or they don't
know what. Gradually, everything will return to normal, I
promise you that. There'll be things for you to write about
in your diary, a fur coat for me, a lavish shoe tree for that other.

     [. . .]

Make that two slices. I can see you only through a vegetal murk
not unlike coral, if it were semi-liquid, or a transparent milkshake.
I have adjusted the lamp,
morning's at seven,
the tarnish has fallen from the metallic embroidery, the walls have fallen,
the country's pulse is racing. Parents are weeping,
the schools have closed.

All the fuss has put me in a good mood,
O great sun.

THEY DON'T JUST GO AWAY, EITHER

In Scandinavia, where snow falls frequently
in winter, then lies around for quite some time,
lucky cousins were living in a time-vault of sorts.
No purchase on the ground floor, but through a funnel-shaped drain
one could catch glimpses, every so often, of the peach-colored
firmament. It's so terrific! It's purer than you think,
too, not that that need unduly concern us.

Father sat in his living room
off the main parlor, working at his table. We never knew
exactly what he did. We kids would amuse ourselves
with games like Authors and Old Maid, until Mamma abruptly
withdrew the lamp, and we all sat shivering in the dark for a while.
Soon it was time to go to bed. We groped our way up
non-existent flights of stairs to the attic funnel.
Everything is so peaceful in here I can dream of more kinds
of things at once. But what if the dreams were prophetic?
Stumbling down an alley, screaming, forehead bathed in blood
or ossified like an old tree root that can barely speak, and when it can,
says things like: "Do you know your horse is on fire?"

Many winters were passed in this way.
I cannot say I feel any wiser for it.
Instead my brain feels like a face freshly shaved
by the barber. I rub it with satisfaction,
giving him a good tip on the way out.
More fanciful patterns await us further along
in our destiny, I tell him, and he agrees; anything
to be rid of me and on to the next customer.
Outside, in the street, a length of silk unspools beautifully,
rejoicing in its doom.

[. . .]

Father, I can go no farther, the lamp blinds me
and the man behind me keeps whispering things in my ear
I'd prefer not to be able to understand . . .
Yet you must, my child, for the sake of the cousins
and the rabbit who await us in the dooryard.

Then I walked on a ways.
It became apparent that the journey (for
such it was) was far from unavoidable.
A twig skewered my sock
and I looked up at the oak tree's strapless trunk,
hoping to escape from what seemed a parable,
from which escape is never possible.

I know *that*. But there is still time for surprises
like the time you looked at me and smiled
just as the sledge was dragging us past a bunker
scented with antique urine. In short

it is here that I shall found a colony
and call it God.

The wasps that night had never been loonier,
making reading impossible. I put down my volume
of *Little Dorrit*, and gnats flung themselves even closer
with propositions. "Hey, how'd you like to be rid of that guy
and us too? All you need do is push a button
and a mandarin somewhere on the other side of the world
will stagger for a moment, seeing his life transpire
before him: that first bowl of gruel, graduation day
at mandarin school, and later on doubts and remorse,
a flummoxed present that seeps into the past,
making a whole life seem regrettable." No,
I cannot condone your offer, the thick answer is for later.
Meanwhile I shall try to pacify my eyeballs
with the mist leaking from the ceiling.

      [. . .]

That proved sufficient, caressing the knocker,
a goblin's face, that drew us back a hundred years
even as it gazed at us in surprise, speechless
as a field of daisies, to a time when we too were out of step
and the whole sentient world offered to bathe us—
pale bluster, flubbing today again and again.

STANZAS BEFORE TIME

Quietly as if it could be
otherwise, the ocean turns
and slinks back into her panties.

Reefs must know something of this,
and all the incurious red fish
that float ditsily in schools,

wondering which school is best.
I'd take you for a drive
in my flivver, Miss Ocean, honest, if I could.

A SUIT

The audience was scattered forever, and the story left untold.
—from the film *Careful,* by Guy Maddin

Maybe it only looks bedraggled.
Let's take it up to the fifth floor and see.
One can look quite far in that light, into the corners
of experiences we never knew we had, that is to say most of them.

But the city is new. The new apartment building, now vacant,
circles like a moth that as yet has no idea
it's trapped in a spider's web, that the indelible
will soon come to pass. For a few moments now
we can drink tea and talk of the famous doll collection
in the museum of a small European spa.
Shadows on the tent alert us: Breathing isn't going to be as easy
as we'd thought once. Mr. Cheeseworth is always so right
in his calculations, yet when one comes to believe him, where is he?

It has been a life of qualification and delay.
Yet we knew we were on the right track; something surged in us,
telling us otherwise, that we'd arrive too early at the airport
or something about the drips on the taxi in the dusk.
We doctored it all up,
and I think I have an explanation for the manna
that falls softly as pollen, and tastes like coconut or some other
unaccountable sherbet. It seems clothes never do fit.

Yes, I could have told you that some time ago.

CROSSROADS IN THE PAST

That night the wind stirred in the forsythia bushes,
but it was a wrong one, blowing in the wrong direction.
"That's silly. How can there be a wrong direction?
'It bloweth where it listeth,' as you know, just as we do
when we make love or do something else there are no rules for."

I tell you, something went wrong there a while back.
Just don't ask me what it was. Pretend I've dropped the subject.
No, now you've got me interested, I want to know
exactly what seems wrong to you, how something could

seem wrong to you. In what way do things get to be wrong?
I'm sitting here dialing my cellphone
with one hand, digging at some obscure pebbles with my shovel
with the other. And then something like braids will stand out,

on horsehair cushions. That armchair is really too lugubrious.
We've got to change all the furniture, fumigate the house,
talk our relationship back to its beginnings. Say, you know
that's probably what's wrong—the beginnings concept, I mean.
I aver there are no beginnings, though there were perhaps some
sometime. We'd stopped, to look at the poster the movie theater

had placed freestanding on the sidewalk. The lobby cards
drew us in. It was afternoon, we found ourselves
sitting at the end of a row in the balcony; the theater was unexpectedly
crowded. That was the day we first realized we didn't fully
know our names, yours or mine, and we left quietly
amid the gray snow falling. Twilight had already set in.

HOW DANGEROUS

Like a summer kangaroo, each of us is a part
of the sun in its tumbling commotion. Like us
it made no move to right things, basking where the spent stream
trickled into the painted grotto.

Yes, and the snow-covered steppe, part of the same opera,
stretched into dimness, awaiting the tenor's aria
of hopelessness. Yet no shadow fell across any of it.
It might have been real. Perhaps it was. Stranger tales
have been spun by travelers in unreassuring inns
while the last embers collapse one into the other, waking
no riposte. "It was at a garrison in central Tadzhikistan."
And then sort of get used to it, and then not be there.

Each noted with pleasure that the other had aged,
realizing as well that new scenery would have to be sent for
and transported thousands of miles over narrow-gauge railroads—

a fountain in a park, a comforting school interior,
a happy hospital—and that, yes, it would be worth waiting for.

And of course one does run on too long,
but whose fault is it? At five dollars
a blip, who's counting? One could, I suppose,
relax one's discourse, not enough
to frighten it, but to have something cold
in the hand, to cool the palm; the words might
then unspool in a different mode, shadow
of an intention behind the screen
before the lights go up and the generals
sidle on for another confab. "It was *you*
who got us involved in this Dreyfus business." "Liar!"
Let's take a commercial break here,
my head is cobwebby from all the facts
that got stuffed into it this afternoon.

In no way am I the island I was yesterday.
Children and small pets rejoice around my ankles;
yellow ribbons come down from the tree trunks.
This is *my* day! Anybody doesn't realize it
is a goddam chameleon or a yes man! Yes, sir,
we'd noticed your singular pallor, singular
even for you. Ambulances have been summoned,
are rumbling across the delta at this moment,
I'd wager. Meanwhile, if there's anything we can do
to make you comfortable for two or three minutes . . .

The heath is ablaze again. Our longest hose
won't come to within four miles of it.
Don't you realize what this means for us,
for our families, our ancestors? The page,
summoned, duly arrived with the wilted asters
someone had mistakenly ordered. It's a variation

on our habitual not-being-able-to-keep-a-straight-face withdrawal,
turning our back on the smoke and blood-red fumes
we already knew were there, plunging out of hedgerows
so dense not even a titmouse could get through.
Never were we to be invited back again, I mean
no one asked me back again. The others sinned too, each
in her different way, and I have the photographs to prove it,
faded to the ultima thule of legibility.
Next time, you write this.

THE UNDERWRITERS

Sir Joshua Lipton drank this tea
and liked it well enough to start selling it
to a few buddies, from the deck of his yacht.

It spread around the world, became a global
kind of thing. Today everybody knows its story,
and we must be careful not to offend our sponsors,
to humor their slightest whims, no matter how insane
they may seem to us at the time. Like the time one of them
wanted all the infants in the burg aged five or under
to be brought before him, wearing rose-colored sashes,
in order that he might read the Book of Job to them all day.
There were, as you may imagine, many tears shed,
flowing and flopping about, but in the end the old geezer
(the sponsor, not Job) was satisfied, and sank into a sleep more delicate
than any the world had ever known. You see what it's like here—
it's a madhouse, Sir, and I am planning to flee the first time
an occasion presents himself, say as a bag of laundry,
or the cargo of a muffin truck. Meanwhile, the "sands"
of time, as they call them, are slipping by with scarcely a whisper
except for the most lynx-eyed among us. We'll make do,

another day, shopping and such, bringing the meat home at night
all roseate and gleaming, ready for the frying pan.
Our names will be read off a roll call we won't hear—
how could we? We're not even born yet—the stars will perform their dance
privately, for us, and the pictures in the great black book
that opens at night will enchant us with their yellow harmonies.
We'll manage to get back, someday, to the tie siding where the idea
of all this began, frustrated and a little hungry, but eager

to hear each others' tales of what went on in the interim
of our long lives, what the tea leaves said
and whether it turned out that way. I'll brush your bangs
a little, you'll lean against my hip for comfort.

VENDANGES

A tall building in the fifteenth arrondissement faded away slowly and then completely vanished. Toward November the weather grew very bitter. No one knew why or even noticed. I forgot to tell you your hat looked perky.

A new way of falling asleep has been discovered. Senior citizens snoop around to impose that sleep. You awake feeling refreshed but something has changed. Perhaps it's the children singing too much. Sophie shouldn't have taken them to the concert. I pleaded with her at the time, to no avail. Also, they have the run of the yard. Someone else might want to use it, or have it be empty. All the chairs were sat on in one night.

And I was pale and restless. The actors walked with me to the cabins. I knew that someone was about to lose or destroy my life's work, or invention. Yet something urged calm on me.

There is an occasional friend left, yes. Married men, hand to mouth. I went down to the exhibition. We came back and listened to some records. Strange, I hadn't noticed the lava pouring. But it's there, she said, every night of the year, like a river. I guess I notice things less now than I used to,

when I was young.

And the arbitrariness of so much of it, like sheep's wool from a carding comb. You can't afford to be vigilant, she said. You must stay this way, always, open and vulnerable. Like a body cavity. Then if you are noticed it will be too late to file the architectural pants. We must, as you say, keep in touch. Not to be noticed. If it was for this I was born, I murmured under my breath. What have I been doing around here, all this month? Waiting for the repairman, I suppose.

Where were you when the last droplets dribbled? Fastening my garter belt to my panty hose. The whole thing was over in less time than you could say Jack Robinson and we were back at base camp, one little thing after another gone wrong, yet on the whole life is spiritual. Still, it is time to pull up stakes. Probably we'll meet a hooded stranger on the path who will point out a direction for us to take, and that will be okay too, interesting even if it's boring.

I remember the world of cherry blossoms looking up at the sun and wondering, what have I done to deserve this or anything else?

Having escaped the first box,
I wandered into a fenced-off arena
from which the distance, peach-blue, could be ascertained:

convenient for my adventures
at this period of my life. Yet I wriggled farther into an indeterminate space
that was actually a mood, or many moods, one overlaying another
like gift wrap.

This is actually what was supposed to take place:
a duet of duelling cuckoos, at the close of which the winner
gets to stand next to me for the photo-op.

Alas, things went terribly wrong.
For I can now claim no space as rightfully mine
and must stand at the edge of the crowd like a ghost
for an unforeseeable length of time.

All this because I meant to be polite to someone.
We had met in the desert, you see, and he wished for a warm place
that wasn't the desert, and I said, "Why not try my hometown?
It's warm in winter. Sometimes."

Days later at the hotel bar I learned his real name
and his reason for wanting to trail me to my so-called hometown,
where I had never felt at home, yet never dreamed
of wishing for another. He said our great-great-grandmothers had been friends
in France, in the time of Marie de Médicis. "In any case
you can't let me down now, now that I've tracked you here
and seen how you actually live."

[. . .]

Was that meant to be a compliment? I suppose not,
yet something in his bright-eyed delivery made me imagine
I'd found a new long-lost friend. "Let's go visit the post office,"
I proposed, and he eagerly assented. Walking the narrow streets
I would never again recognize, I got this wistful feeling,
like a long, slow song sung from the tip of a distant tower.
I'd been rejected again, yet how? Nothing had really happened.
My friend was looking straight ahead, not saying anything.

"Is this the place you wanted to come to?
It's not much, I know. Terrazzo floor, frosted panes, a bit of brass
handle here and there, like a handle on a bedpost."

"What's that supposed to mean," he said, and sighed.
"Tomorrow I must be in Ottawa.
I'd hoped to spend the whole day with you, but now it's getting dark
and my bus will be leaving shortly." How could he do this to me?
Easily enough, apparently. "But what about Marie de Médicis?"
I stammered, as the mist broke and then reformed its ranks.
"Shucks, there's not much you can do in Ottawa on a Tuesday."
"That's what you think," came the curt reply. Now all is darkness.

STRANGE CINEMA

In sooth, I come here sadly,
not trembling, not against my will,
hoping you will set the record straight.
You can, you know, in a minute
if the wind is right and no felon intervenes.

And we sit and you tell me how crazy I am.
I shall petition the other board members
but am afraid nothing will ever come right.
It has been going on too long for this to happen,
yet it was right to go, to go on as it did,
even if there was a strangeness in the rightness
that no one can now see. They see the night
in its undress, plaits unplaited, brushed,
the sound of the surf churning on distant rocks,
can think only about how heavenly it would have been
if it had all happened later or differently.

Now, according to some sources,
new retrofitting trends are a commodity,
along with silence, and sweetness.
Doucement, doucement . . .

And when the sweetness is adjusted,
why, we'll know more than some do now.
That is all I can offer you,
my lost, my loved one.

Continually detouring among the mountains,
some got lost, bathed in freshets.
Others stumbled onto the fringes of a large city
just as revolt was breaking out. Tourists, they were told,
should not try to escape, but enjoy the genuine hospitality
of the country, its superior hotels, some with rooms facing the ocean,
all provided with the latest in fitness equipment.
"Sure, try to put a good face on it, make nice with the natives
staring at us. I wonder when the bars open, or if they do."

Back at the Hotel Frisson the mood was one
of subdued reproach, such as a tardy guest feels, even
after apologies have been made and accepted.
Metallic fronds brushed against the catwalks.
Every so often a child would come, always silent,
with simple gifts in her hands, like a rabbit eraser.

This couldn't quite compare with real life though,
as we thought we had experienced it in the past,
even the very recent past. The monsoon, striking at five,
just as elaborate drinks were at last being served,
canceled civility, forcing huge residents to flee.

PASTILLES FOR THE VOYAGE

If it is spring it matters a little,
or not. Some are running down
to get into their cars, shoving
old ladies out of the way. I say,
dude, it made more sense a while ago
when we was on the grass. Tell it to the Ages,
that's what they're there for. You know,
miscellaneous record-keeping, and the like,
the starving of fools
and transformation of opera singers
into the characters they're supposed to be onstage.
Here comes Tosca, chattering with Isolde
about some vivacious bird's egg winter left behind.

I turn the corner into my street
and see them all, all the things that have mattered
to me during my long life: the dung-beetle
who was convinced he could tap dance; the grocer's boy
(he hasn't changed much in eighty years, nor have I);
and the amorphous crowd in black T-shirts with names like
slumlords or slumgullion spattered over them. O my friends
(for I have no other), the beginning of fermentation is *here*,
right on this sidewalk or whatever you call it.
We know, they say, and keep going.
If only I could get the tears out of my eyes it would be raining now.
I must try the new, fluid approach.

But how can I be in this bar and also be a recluse?
The colony of ants was marching toward me, stretching
far into the distance, where they were as small as ants.
Their leader held up a twig as big as a poplar.
It was obviously supposed to be for me.
But he couldn't say it, with a poplar in his mandibles.
Well, let's forget that scene and turn to one in Paris.
Ants are walking down the Champs-Elysées
in the snow, in twos and threes, conversing,
revealing a sociability one never supposed them as having.
The larger ones have almost reached the allegorical statues
of French cities (is it?) on the Place de la Concorde.
"You see, I told you he was going to bolt.
Now he just sits in his attic
ordering copious *plats* from a nearby restaurant
as though God had meant him to be quiet."
"While you are like a portrait of Mme de Staël by Overbeck,
that is to say a little serious and washed out.
Remember you can come to me anytime
with what is bothering you, just don't ask for money.
Day and night my home, my hearth are open to you,
you great big adorable one, you."

The bar was unexpectedly comfortable.
I thought about staying. There was an alarm clock on it.
Patrons were invited to guess the time (the clock was always wrong).
More cheerful citizenry crowded in, singing the Marseillaise,
congratulating each other for the wrong reasons, like the color
of their socks, and taking swigs from a communal jug.
"I just love it when he gets this way,
which happens in the middle of August, when summer is on its way
out, and autumn is still just a glint in its eye,

a chronicle of hoar-frost foretold."
"Yes and he was going to buy all the candy bars in the machine
but something happened, the walls caved in (who knew
the river had risen rapidly?) and one by one people were swept away
calling endearing things to each other, using pet names.
'Achilles, meet Angus.' " Then it all happened so quickly I
guess I never knew where we were going, where the pavement
was taking us.

Things got real quiet in the oubliette.
I was still reading *Jean-Christophe*. I'll never finish the darn thing.
Now is the time for you to go out into the light
and congratulate whoever is left in our city. People who survived
the eclipse. But I was totally taken with you, always have been.
Light a candle in my wreath, I'll be yours forever and will kiss you.

from CHINESE WHISPERS

(2002)

A NICE PRESENTATION

I have a friendly disposition but am forgetful, though I tend to forget only important things. Several mornings ago I was lying in my bed listening to a sound of leisurely hammering coming from a nearby building. For some reason it made me think of spring which it is. Listening I heard also a man and woman talking together. I couldn't hear very well but it seemed they were discussing the work that was being done. This made me smile, they sounded like good and dear people and I was slipping back into dreams when the phone rang. No one was there.

Some of these are perhaps people having to do with anything in the world. I wish to go away, on a dark night, to leave people and the rain behind but am too caught up in my own selfish thoughts and desires for this. For it to happen I would have to be asleep and already started on my voyage of self-discovery around the world. One is certain then to meet many people and to hear many strange things being said. I like this in a way but wish it would stop as the unexpectedness of it conflicts with my desire to revolve in a constant, deliberate motion. To drink tea from a samovar. To use chopsticks in the land of the Asiatics. To be stung by the sun's bees and have it not matter.

Most things don't matter but an old woman of my acquaintance is always predicting doom and gloom and her prophecies matter though they may never be fulfilled. That's one reason I don't worry too much but I like to tell her she is right but also wrong because what she says won't happen. Yet how can I or anyone know this? For the seasons do come round in leisurely fashion and one takes a pinch of something from each, according to one's desires and what it leaves behind. Not long ago I was in a quandary about this but now it's too late. The evening comes on and the aspens leaven its stars. It's all about this observatory a shout fills.

After my fall from the sixteenth floor my bones were lovingly assembled. They were transparent. I was carried into the gorgeous dollhouse and placed on a fainting couch upholstered with brilliant poppies. My ship had come in, so to speak.

There were others, lovers, sitting and speaking nearby. "Are you the Countess of C?" I demanded. She smiled and returned her gaze to the other. Someone brought in a tray of cakes which were distributed to the guests according to a fixed plan. "Here, this one's for you. Take it." I looked and saw only a small cat rolling in the snow of the darkened gutter. "If this is mine, then I don't want it." Abruptly the chords of a string quartet finished. I was on a shallow porch. The village movie palaces were letting out. I thought I saw a cousin from years back. Before I could call out she turned, sallow. I saw that this was not the person. Conversations continued streaming in the erstwhile twilight, I betook myself to the tollbooth. The pumpkin-yellow sun lit all this up, climbing slowly from ankles to handlebar.

He had shaved his head some seven years ago. The lovers were bored then. They no longer meandered by the brook's side, telling and retelling ancient secrets, as though this time of life were an anomaly, a handicap that had been foreseen. "In truth these labels don't go far. It was I who made a career in singing, but it could just as well have been somewhere else."

Indeed? The dust was sweeping itself up, making sport of the broom. The solar disk was clogged with the bristles of impending resolution. Which direction did he say to take? I'm confused now, a little. It was my understanding we would in joining hands be chastised, that the boss man would be sympathetic, the sly apprentice unresonant as a squatter's tree house. See though, it wasn't me that dictated . . .

that dictated the orbits of the plants, the viburnum at the door. And just as I had called to you, the image decomposed. Restlessness of fish in a deodorant ad. By golly, Uncle Ted will soon be here. Until it happens you can catch your breath, looking about the walls of the familiar nest. But his flight was delayed for five hours. *Now* someone was interested. The travel mishaps of others are truly absorbing. He read from a large timetable and the helium balloon rose straight up out of the city, entered the region of others' indifference and their benighted cares. Can't that child be made to stop practicing?

In another life we were in a cottage made of thin boards, above a small lake. The embroidered hems of waves annoyed the shoreline. There were no boats, only trees and boathouses.

It's good to step off that steel carousel. The woods were made for musicianly echoes, though not all at once. Too many echoes are like no echo, or a single tall one. Please return dishes to main room after using. Try a little subtlety in self-defense; it'll help, you'll find out.

The boards of the cottage grew apart and we walked out into the sand under the sea. It was time for the sun to exhort the mute apathy of sitters, hangers-on. Ballast of the universal dredging operation. The device was called candy. We had seen it all before but would never let on, not until the postman came right up to the door, borne on the noble flood. Racked by jetsam, we cry out for flotsam, anything to stanch the hole in the big ad.

We all came to be here quite naturally. You see we are the lamplighters of our criminal past, trailing red across the sidewalks and divided highways. Yes, she said, you most certainly can come here now and be assured of staying, of starving, forever if we wish, though we shall not observe the dark's convolutions much longer (sob). Utterly you are the under one, we are all neighbors if you wish, but don't under any circumstances go crawling to the barrel organ for sympathy, you would only blow a fuse and where's the force in that? I know your seriousness is long gone, facing pink horizons in other hemispheres. We'd all blow up if it didn't. Meanwhile it's nice to have a chair. A chair is a good thing to be. We should all know that.

The last trail unspools beyond Ohio.

Dickhead, they called him, for his name was Dong, Tram Van Dong. Carefully he slid open the small judas in his chest and withdrew a heart-shaped disk. It appeared to be cut from thicknesses of newspaper crudely stapled together. There was handwriting on one side, "spirit writing," he indicated with a motion of his head. Yet it all seemed for naught, ancient stock-market quotations or chalked messages on hoardings of the last century, with plus and minus signs featured prominently. "*O vos omnes*," he breathed, "blown together like milkweed on the hither shore of this embattled plain, will your feet soon mean to you what once they did? I think not. Meanwhile the tempest brays, favor is curried, the taffetas of autumn slide toward us over the frosted parquet, and this loquat heart is yours for the dividing. Sailboat of the Luxembourg! Vibrations of crisp mornings ripple ever closer, the joiner joins, the ostler ostles, the seducer seduces, nor stirs far from his crimson hammock. Delphic squibs caparison the bleak afternoon and the critics love it, eat it up, can't get enough of it. 'More pap! More pap!' Have a care, though, lest what I tell you here trespass beyond the booth of our conniving. Yet it will spread, as surely as an epidemic becomes the element we have chosen to live in: our old infectious experiment."

FROM THE DIARY OF A MOLE

Shoehorning in one's own tribute to crustiness is another life-form for him. Something then went out of us. In the pagan dawn three polar bears stand in the volumetric sky's grapeade revelation.

"Time to go to the thoughtful house."

They may not get you here, they may not get you there, they may not get you everywhere, but they will get you somewhere. Yet the proposition never came to a vote, was not voted on. You see the realism in it? No, of course you don't, for something else is still there, something to replace all of it in one block. Anent the spillway: His crimes are gorgeous but don't matter just now. Later

we will call him on them. When it subsides. That is, everything.

Just a teardrop of milk, thanks. Don't believe that rag. It inferred we were adolescents, once, that sex roared over us like a mudslide, leaving us. We were lost. So lost, in fact, that his mother didn't know me till I came out toward her, and she knew me and was not afraid, was glad in fact, for the rainbow late in the day in its foam of cloud, poised above the basin. Then I had a preshrunk sweater sent to him and asked if there was anything else. "Nothing, a fresh breeze." Still, leaves are asleep. The bears act as if no one's there. She curls up in the curlew's nest, weeping on its golden eggs. It took the savagery of centuries of animal conflict to bring us just short of this, and you, why have you done? Oh, I

don't much matter I guess. If that's all I'll be on my way. To the box in which savage handwriting is hidden, too dense for you to decipher, too lorn for a world to unravel just now, but like they say I'll be suing you. So really it's fine until Christmas I can stand it, a runt, I'll just go on blooming in my box, unaware of things sleeping pagans say about us, glad to crash, collapse the silk hat, garden's done and I'm all in and breathless for a breather. Come right in. What world is this.

MORDRED

Now I have neither back nor front.
I am the way certain persons are
who never tell you how they are
yet you know they are like you and they are.

I was preternaturally wise
but it was spring, there was no one to care or do.
It was spring and the sprinklers were on.

Bay, indentation, viscous rocks
that are somebody's pleasure. Pleasures that don't go away
but don't exactly stay,
stay the way they were meant to be.
I caught a winged one,
looked it firmly in the eyes:
What is your surmise? Oh, I only like living on,
the rest isn't so important to me,
not at all, if you wish.
But I do, I said. Then, well, it's like a clearing
in the darkness that you can't see. Darkness is meant for all of us.
We grow used to it. Then daylight comes again.
That's what I mean when I say about living
it could be going on, going somewhere else,
but it's not, it's here, more or less.
You have to champion it, then it fights for you,
but that isn't necessary. It will go on living anyway.
I say do you mind I'm getting tired.

But there is one last thing I must know about you.
Do you remember a midnight forge
around which crept the ghosts of lepers, who were blacksmiths
in a time persistently unidentifiable, and then you went like this?

You remember how the hammer fell slowly
taking all that song with you.
You remember the music of the draft horses
they could only make against a wall.
All right, how little does it all cost you then?
You were a schoolchild, now you are past middle age,
and the great drawing hasn't occurred.

I see I must be going.
I just like living,
only like living.
Sometime you must tell me of your intentions,
but now I have to stay here on this fast track
in case the provisions come along
which I won't need, being a living, breathing creature.
But I asked you about your hat.
Oh yes well it is important to have a hat.

THE LIGHTNING CONDUCTOR

The general was always particular about his withers,
lived in a newspaper tent
someone had let fall beside an easy chair.
Telling the man with no fingers what it was like to smoke a cigarette
in the Twenties, we proceeded naturally to your cousin Junius.
His plan was to overtake the now speeding tortoise
by digging some kind of a fire trench in its path,
which would cause it to wonder,
fatally, for a second,
after which we could all go back to channeling the news.
There's a story here about a kind of grass that grows in the Amazon
valley that is too tall for birds to fly over—
they fly past it instead—
yet leeches have no trouble navigating its circuitous heaps
and are wont to throw celebratory banquets afterward,
at which awards are given out—best costume in a period piece
too distracted by the rapids to notice what period it is, and so on.
Before retiring the general liked to play a game of all-white dominoes,
after which he would place his nightcap distractedly on the other man's crocheted
     chamber-pot lid.
Subsiding into fitful slumber, warily he dreams
of the giant hand descended from heaven
like the slope of a moraine, whose fingers were bedizened with rings
in which every event that had ever happened in the universe could sometimes be
     discerned.

Sometimes you end up in a slough no matter what happens,
no matter how many precautions have been taken, threads picked from the tapestry
that was to have provided us with underwear, and now is bare as any
grassless season, on whatever coast you choose to engage.
It's sad that many were left behind,

but a good thing for the bluebirds in their beige houses.
They never saw any reason to join the vast, confused migration,
fucking like minks as far as the spotty horizon.
It doesn't get desperately cold any more, and that's certainly a lucky anomaly too.

I ASKED MR. DITHERS WHETHER
IT WAS TIME YET HE SAID NO TO WAIT

Time, you old miscreant! Slain any brontosauruses lately? You—
Sixty wondering days I watched him navigate the alkali lick,
always a little power ebbing, streaming from high windowsills.
Down here the tetched are lonely. There's nothing they can do
except spit.

We felt better about answering the business letter
once the resulting hubris had been grandfathered in,
slowly, by a withered sage in clogs
and a poncho vast as a delta, made of some rubbery satinlike
material. It was New Year's Eve
again. Time to get out the punch bowl,
make some resolutions,
I don't think.

And in a little while we broke under the strain:
suppurations ad nauseam, the wanting to be taller,
though it's simply about being mysterious, i.e., not taller,
like any tree in any forest.
                Mute, the pancake describes you.
It had tiny Roman numerals embedded in its rim.
It was a pancake clock. They had 'em in those days,
always getting smaller, which is why they finally became extinct.
It was a hundred years before anyone noticed.
                    The governor-general
called it "sinuous." But we, we had other names for it,
knew it was going to be around for a long time,
even though extinct. And sure as shillelaghs fall from trees
onto frozen doorsteps, it came round again
when all memory of it had been expunged
                        from the common brain.
Everybody wants to try one of those new pancake clocks.
A boyfriend in the next town had one
but conveniently forgot to bring it over each time we invited him.
Finally the rumors grew more fabulous than the real thing:
I hear they are encrusted with tangles of briar rose,
                  so dense
not even a prince seeking the Sleeping Beauty could get inside.
What's more, there are more of them than when they were extinct,
yet the prices keep on rising. They have them in the Hesperides
and in shantytowns on the edge of the known world,
blue with cold. All downtowns used to feature them.
                    Camera obscuras,
too, were big that year. But why is it that with so many people
who want to know what a shout is about, nobody can find the original recipe?

All too soon, no one cares. We go back to doing little things for each other,
pasting stamps together to form a tiny train track, and other,
less noticeable things. The past is forgotten till next time.
How to describe the years? Some were like blocks of the palest halvah,
careless of being touched. Some took each other's trash out,
put each other's eyes out. So many got thrown out
before anyone noticed, it was like a chiaroscuro

                                        of collapsing clouds.
How I longed to visit you again in that old house! But you were deaf,
or dead. Our letters crossed. A motorboat was ferrying me out past
the reef, people on shore looked like dolls fingering stuffs.

                                                More
keeps coming out about the dogs. Surely a simple embrace
from an itinerant fish would have been spurned at certain periods. Not now.
There's a famine of years in the land, the women are beautiful,
but prematurely old and worn. It doesn't get better. Rocks half-buried
in bands of sand, and spontaneous execrations.

                                        I yell to the ship's front door,
wanting to be taller, and somewhere in the middle all this gets lost.
I was a phantom for a day. My friends carried me around with them.

It always turns out that much is salvageable.
                                        Chicken coops
haven't floated away on the flood. Lacemakers are back in business
with a vengeance. All the locksmiths had left town during the night.
It happened to be a beautiful time of season, spring or fall,
the air was digestible, the fish tied in love knots
on their gurneys. Yes, and journeys

were palpable too: Someone had spoken of saving appearances
and the walls were just a little too blue in mid-morning.
Was there ever such a time? I'd like to handle you,

bruise you with kisses for it, yet something always stops me short:
the knowledge that this isn't history,

                                        no matter how many
times we keep mistaking it for the present, that headlines
trumpet each day. But behind the unsightly school building, now a pickle
warehouse, the true nature of things is known, is not overridden:
Yours is a vote like any other. And there is fraud at the ballot boxes,
stuffed with lace valentines and fortunes from automatic scales,
dispensed with a lofty kind of charity, as though this could matter
to us, these tunes
                        carried by the wind
from a barrel organ several leagues away. No, this is not the time
to reveal your deception to us. Wait till rain and old age
have softened us up a little more.
                                        Then we'll see how extinct
the various races have become, how the years stand up
to their descriptions, no matter how misleading,
and how long the disbanded armies stay around. I must congratulate you
on your detective work, for I am a connoisseur
of close embroidery, though I don't have a diploma to show for it.

The trees, the barren trees, have been described more than once.
Always they are taller, it seems, and the river passes them
without noticing. We, too, are taller,
our ceilings higher, our walls more tinctured
with telling frescoes, our dooryards both airier and vaguer,
according as time passes and weaves its minute deceptions in and out,
a secret thread.
Peace is a full stop.
And though we had some chance of slipping past the blockade,
now only time will consent to have anything to do with us,
for what purposes we do not know.

IN THE TIME OF PUSSY WILLOWS

This is going to take some time.
Nope, it's almost over. For today anyway.
We'll have a beautiful story, old story
to fish for as his gasps come undone.

I never dreamed the pond of chagrin
would affect me this much. Look, I'm shaking,
shrinking with the devil
in the stagy sunrise he devised.
Then there will be no letters for what is truth,
to make up the words of it. It will be standing still
for all it's worth. A hireling shepherd came along,
whistling, his eyes on the trees. He was a servant of two masters,
which is some excuse, although not really all that much of a one.
Anyway, he overstayed his welcome. The last train had already left.

How does one conduct one's life amid such circumstances,
dear snake, who want the best for us
as long as you're not hurt by it?
My goodness, I thought I'd seen a whole lot of generations,
but they are endless, one keeps following another,
treading on its train, hissing.

What a beautiful old story it could be after all
if those in the back rows would stop giggling for a minute.
By day, we paddled and arbitraged
to get to this spot. By night it hardly matters.
Strange we didn't anticipate this,
but the dumbest clues get overlooked by the smartest gumshoe
and we're back in some fetishist's vinyl paradise
with no clue as to how we got here
except the tiny diamond on your pillow—it must have been a tear

hatched from a dream, when you actually knew what you were doing.
Now, it's all fear. Fear and wrongdoing.
Our outboard motor sputters and quits, and silence
beats down from every point in the sky. To have digested this
when we were younger, and felt a set of balls coming on . . .
It may be that thunder and lightning are two-dimensional,
that there was never really any place for fear,
that others get trapped, same as us, and make up
amusing stories to cover their tracks. Wait,
there's one in the donjon wants to speak his piece. Rats,
now he's gone too.

Yes, he slipped and died in front of you,
and you intend to twist this into an ethos?
Go make up other stories.
Window reflected in the bubble,
how often I've tried to pray to you,
but your sphere would have nothing of it.
I felt almost jinxed. Then a spider led the way
back into the room

and I knew why we'd never left. Outside was brushfires.
Here was the peace of Philemon and Baucis,
offering chunks of bread and salami to the tattered stranger,
and a beaker of wine darker than the deepest twilight,
a table spread with singularities
for the desperate and tragic among us.

Angel, come back please. Let us smell your heavenly smell again.

LITTLE SICK POEM

If living is a hate crime, so be it.
But hey—I was around when they invented the Cardiff giant.
I kid you not. God wanted you to know,
so you'd remember to love Him. Yes, He often confides in me,

tips me off to the whereabouts of valuable junk
but doesn't want me to let on we are in cahoots.
This lamp, covered in rust, is valuable
though not old. It is collectible,
as we all are, in a sense. I love you,
it's sexual harassment, but we get on that way,
through bluster, through dried open fields.

If I were you I'd get an unlisted number,
then think about growing up, just a little.
I can't tell you which divining bones to choose, that's your job,
and when you come close, I wish it was all around,

around over me. The jingle of your hat comforts me,
confirms me in my worst aspects. I shall never be anything but a clown,
now. And there's so much work to do,
so many puzzles to ignore.

LOCAL LEGEND

Arriving late at the opera one night
I ran into Dr. Gradus ad Parnassum hastening down the marble stair,
swan-like. "I wouldn't bother if I was you," he confided.
"It's a Verdi work written before he was born.
True, his version of the Faust legend is unique:
Faust tempts Mephistopheles to come up with something
besides the same old shit. Finally, at his wit's end, the devil
urges Valentine to take his place, promising him big rewards
this side of Old Smoky. Then, wouldn't you know, Gretchen gets involved.
They decide to make it into a harassment case. No sooner
does Faust hit the street than the breeze waffles his brow,
he can't say where he came from, or if he ever had a youth
to be tempted back into."
                              The bats arrived. It was their moment.
Twenty million bats fly out of an astonishingly low culvert
every night, in season. I kid you not. After a cursory swoop
or two, they all fly back in. It all happens in a matter of
minutes, seconds, almost. Which reminds me, have you chosen your second?
Mephisto wants you to use this foil. It works better.
No, there's nothing wrong with it.

Hours later I stood with the good doctor
in a snow-encrusted orchard. He urged the value
of mustard plasters on me. "See, it makes sense."
Yet we both knew they are poisonous in some climates,
though only if taken in minute quantities.

See you again, old thing.

We were reading to ourselves. Sometimes to others.
I was quietly reading the margin
when the doves fell, it was blue
outside. Perhaps in a moment,
he said. The moment never came.
I was reading something else now,
it didn't matter. Other people came and
dropped off their résumés. I wasn't being idle,
exactly. Someone wanted to go away
altogether in this preposterous season.

Too bad he never tried it—
he might have liked it.

She saw us make eye contact.
And that was that for that day.

Too bad he too, when I
am

meaning if I came along it'd
already be too late.

Some of the swans are swarming.
The spring has gone under—it wasn't
supposed to be like this.

Now they watch him and cringe.
Who are they? Who is he?

We decided to fly Chinese.
The food wasn't that good.

And oh Erwin did I tell you
that man—the one—I didn't

know if I was supposed to or not.
He crawled back listlessly,

holding a bunch of divas.
It's hard work getting these out,

    [. . .]

but so's any thing you're entitled to do:
classes to attend.

The morning of school.
Evening almost over,

they bend the security rules.
It's time for another fog bomb.

Lookit the way they all roost.
Poor souls clashed together

until almost the root's roof
separates us from our beginning.

We slew many giants in our day,
burned many libraries.

Roundabouts, swings,
it was all one piece of luck to us.

Now we're washed up it's almost cold.
Not bad enough to put up a stand.

Out of that longing we built a paean.
Now everyone who crosses this bridge is wiser.

It doesn't tilt much.
Look, the shore is arriving laterally.

    [. . .]

Some people literally think they know a lot,
gets 'em in trouble, we must rake out

cafés looking for rats and exploded babies.
There was one too many last week.

I don't know if you're coding.
The cop pulled us over

in a shawl. Why do you want to go around me
when there are other circulars

to be had for the looking?
I never thought about being grounded forever.

This is Mademoiselle. Take your hat off.
There's no need, I was here last Thursday.

All the best creatures are thwarted
for their pains. He removed my chains deftly,

processed my passport with gunk.
Now two times five geese fly across

the crescent moon, it is time to get down to
facts, in the tiny park.

There were priests posing as nuns,
quinces and stuff.

Tilt me a little more to the sun,
I want to see it one last time. There,

[. . .]

that's just fine, I've seen it.
You can roll me inside. On wings of what perturbation?

He came for the julep.
He was gone in an instant.

We cry too much over
drowned dogs.

He came in last week too.
Said he knew you or somebody else.

It's the pain just of replying
that makes so many of them take up different lines.

Too many goods—we are spoiled indeed.
Had we learned to subsist on less

the changing of the world might be different,
earth come to greet us. I say, the chairs have grown back.

The couple sat in the dish drainer
pondering an uncertain future.

The kitchen had never looked bleaker
except for two chinchillas near the stove, a beaker

of mulled claret, shaving soap smelling
so fresh and new, like smoke, almost.

     [. . .]

He says leave it here,
that he comes here.

OK harness the DeSoto,
we'll have other plans

for newness, for a renewing, kind of—
picnics in the individual cells

so no one falls asleep for it, dreams
she is a viola, instrument of care, of sorts.

You should have seen him when we got back.
He was absolutely wild. Hadn't wanted us to go

to the picture show. But in a way it was all over,
we were back, the harm had been done.

Gradually he came to realize this
over a period of many years, spanning

two world wars and a major depression.
After that it was time to get up and go,

but who had the get up and go? A child's
party, painted paper hats, bowlfuls of lemonade,

no more at the lemonade stand, it sold out.
That was cheerful. A man came right up behind you,

he had two tickets to the door.
We need starve no more

[. . .]

but religion is elastic too—
might want some at some future date—

if so you'll find it here.
We have to hurry in now,

hurry away, it's the same thing
she said as rain came and stole the king.

OH EVENINGS

The man standing there, the other stranger,
slips easily into the background
as though stopping were the last thing on his mind.

Another, lacking the courage of his convictions,
went mad from drinking seawater. That was an absolute rout.

Oh evenings! Learning where to look it up
became an end in itself. To this purpose
trained fleas were engaged to do sums.
Ants on their way to happiness paused
over the numbers: Did it seem like three
or was it just three? Is this where I came in?

More likely we all need to be blessed for the hole
in his savage argument. Surely, passing through town,
we contributed a little to the regional economy,
received credit for showing our faces.
So what if the only theater in town
had been turned into a funeral parlor?
There are few things more theatrical than death,
one supposes, though one doesn't know.

Which brings me to my original argument.
Ah, what was the argument? Keeping our places,
assuming no more credit than what is due
our tame luster, our positive shine. Then people will go out
into the city, spreading germs, living like it was last year.

RUNWAY

We crawled out of the car
into the rest stop. Lady Baltimore cake
was served by Madame du Barry look-alikes.
"Don't hurry, Mr. Executioner," one chirped,
pressing the unwanted crumbs against my lips.
"It'll all be over in a second," she added encouragingly.

Red Skelton asked me if I had a book coming out. He seemed drowned
in lists of trivia and itching-powder dreams—
the kind that make you wake up
and then sort of fall back into sleep again.
His brother was cleaning up after the elephants. He
wore a crisp white uniform. Could have been a soda jerk,
or just a jerk. My scented glove offends
the daintiest among them, for they have no recourse
but cries of old London—an exhaustive repertory,
one first thought, but soon its coda reared—
a clutch of mordant shrieks.

I supposed it was the witching hour.
Nothing unusual happened. Soon we were leaving home
forever, to be pitched about on storm-tossed seas,
flagrant to be back amid multiple directions. For though there are some
who can live without compasses, it dissolves all complexity
if one is perpetually in the know. Sleep, directions—that's all
I need at my chaste fireside, to take in the sights,
just as the wind starts and darkness longs
to take us down a peg.

The way you look tonight
is perishable, unphotographable, laughable. Sometimes
dyslexia strikes in late middle age. You are
the way I look tonight. *At last*
my love has come along.
And you are mine at last.
Slowly the orchestra wives pick over the set,
go behind a wall. The big smiley man is thinking,
thinking he has an IDEA! Well, if he says so.
You gotta believe him. One orchestra wife comes back.
She has forgotten her pearls. The orchestra riffs around,
they come back. "Well, I never! Of all things!"
Oh, it plays

to the breach. You see it. Her lover and best friend came
along the hall. "I'm sorry, Dan.
But I just couldn't." So it's all alright,
he thinks. He thinks it's a secret.

THE HAVES

Many there were that.
There were many who that.
Many did that to what.
Many undid that to what.
Many there were worse than that.
To undo that many did that.
More of an obstacle to this than that
where the upcoming is done to that.

The undone is done is that.
They are speaking to what is done
not left on the stove.
The done is that to that done.

There were many who did this and that,
meanwhile were many who undid that.
The undone undid the that.
The crisis under the batter's hat.

Do you manage a common if?
If so why is the crisis that?
Who did the crisis there?
Why is the crisis after my time that.

Ordinarily men go around
seeking wedgies the corner is out.
They this and why and in this bat
an eyelash to be better than that
on the day that.

     [. . .]

And that was all a better than that day had that
unto the jousting which was unto a way down that.
They mortared the way under the man hat
that wanted to under a bill be that that.

In London just now is cold.
In London just now a gull spring
in London on the back of the bat
in London on the back of that.

When they and London remove the bat back
the bat backer became the bat back.
The butt packer begat the back pack
under lest the noise disturb those that bat back.

In the backing the true bat resides
under a cleft the cliff nose
gannets nosed underside.
The cliff-size size briar sizes up size,
decides size is lies under briar thighs.

That was a lot of that and lack
come down the stair decorum
and lack of reasonable store bin
under the store the straw was been.
Me like methink it all past being
and beyond into the been that he sinned,
the being that has seen
under the hedgerow greens as feline
is opposed to oppressed being been
and never two of us no no more we'll have been.
     [. . .]

The barn exploded.
The big store ripped apart.
Gravel on the lawn made its mark
yes that and festoon of grit in the sky
while the riders came riding by
and nobody was appointed to fill the exam
no others why no other have ever been
why the irritated sky
and we'll never be the fly
not two states ever to fly by

and no more store no more in store by the fly
they fly by and take just as your daddy did
and stand by the chest

just make sure to be to the thigh
came crawling across clock's tempest.

LIKE AIR, ALMOST

It comes down to
so little:
the gauzy syntax
of one thing and another;
a pleasant dinner
and a frozen train ride into the exhaustible
resources.

We'd had almost enough,
tossing the cap to first one
and then the other one,
but still weren't determined
to give up the drive.
It had so much we wanted!
But besides that, was
fickle, overdetermined.

So I passed on that.
It was worth it.
Angelic eventide came along after afternoon,
a colibri fluttered questioning wings,
all so we might be taken out,
aired.

And when the post-climax happened
in soft shards, falling
this way and that,
signing the night's emeralds away,
we took it to be a sign of something.
"Must be a sign of something."
Then the wind came on, and winter with it.
"Why, weren't we just here,

five minutes ago?"
I thought I'd have another look,
but that way is all changed, and besides,
no one goes there anymore,
it's too popular.

Just one fragment
is all I ever wanted,
but I can have it, it's too much,
but its touch is for another time,
when I'm ready.

Crowd ebbs peacefully.
Hey it's all right.

THE BLESSED WAY OUT

Those who came closest did not come close.
The unknown leaned out to them,
then it was post-afternoon. Yes, Jerry built it.
There are many of them in Old Town.

What with one thing and another
you gave me all sorts of fur presents, you know.
It was good to come back. Gumball machines furnish
the library's stark living style.

You can't compete with what the
car tells its owner. One by one you are mortal ·
if the watershed idea catches on
and if we are credited for our utterance.

They thought serendipity was the most beautiful thing in the world.
They were right. As the wheel takes hold,
other inspirations spike it.

There was no year like it for taxation.
FDR decreed a large public works program
that had to be supported with funds from somewhere.
Inevitably, these took the form of taxation.

As when a redbreast calls, there is someone to hear it.
Calico got pasted over the mouse hole.
What are we doing in a theater more than one
wondered. Leaves fled like falling stocks.

THE BUSINESS OF FALLING ASLEEP (2)

Par délicatesse j'ai perdu ma vie.
—RIMBAUD

Days, things, times of day. Big things like unseen bells. Unheard moments. Suburbs are pale orange and a greenish blue I associate with fire escapes and school. The school looms now: a person with five questions at its back. They can't stay there, for now. They'll be back.

The interrogation was like a question mark. Once you stop to listen you're hooked. No, go back to the stone please. What did it say over the stone? Don't say I can't remember, you remember everything. That is true but I'll remember the stone

like the face of only the third dead person I'd ever seen. Well it's happened, he seemed to be saying. The eyes were closed (I suppose they always are). What are you going to do now? We don't have to stay like this. We could meet perhaps outside. Have a tea like we used to.

They moved the hotel boat to a less ostentatious location, still it felt hard coming to you through trees and other animated life. "Its music doesn't gel." Yes, but a weird creepy feeling came over me that you might know about all this, not wanted to tell me but just know. It's amazing how the past shrinks to the size of your palm, forced to hold all that now. Falling down the steps in Marlborough Street. That was just one thing, but others I don't know, never will know, are cupped in the hand as well. To brave the day turning outward like an ear, too polite to hear.

Rimbaud said it well, though his speech could be clamorous. One accepts that too within a broader parterre of accepting, a load of sun coming over the house to dampen discreet despair, woven into the togs of somebody standing up to go having remarked on the time as though there were a time to go. One would rather be left with few words and the resulting remainder of unease than never to have left the party.

[. . .]

Visions of a terrace with a cell phone ought to be engraved on the waiting skull, like Brahms. Anxious in the predicate but adept socially, pressure to have the music come out in a certain place, where it can be abandoned if desired. How about it? I care too much

not to leave it all. Set this down too . . .

SIR GAMMER VANS

Last Sunday morning at six o'clock in the evening as I was sailing
over the tops of the mountains in my little boat a crew-cut stranger
saluted me, so I asked him, could he tell me whether the little old
woman was dead yet who

was hanged last Saturday week for drowning herself in a shower of feathers?
"Ask Monk Lewis what he thinks 'been there done that' means in the so-called
evening of life. Chances are he'll regale you with chess moves. All I
want is my damn prescription." "And you shall have it, *sir*," he answered
in a level voice. So he gave me a slice of beer and a cup of cold veal
and there was this little dog.

I see no reason to be more polite when the sun has passed its zenith,
yet ham radio operators infest every cove, defacing walls with their palaver.
And when two swans come to that, one swoons and is soothed.
The other lost inside a wall.

He seemed to think I knew some secret or other pertaining to the botched
logs in the fireplace. This caused him to avoid me I think
for a twelvemonth.
After which we got down to business and actually signed the contract.
He was inconsolable. The brat had cost him. With two wives and another
on the way wouldn't commit himself to a used Chevy. Which is
understandable I think I said it's understandable. The man
was in no mood to entertain these distinctions. At least I thought he said
bring on the heavy artillery the dream is now or
it won't happen, not in my diary. Well why that's just what
I think too, I blessed him. Cells in the wind. The sucker'll be all
over our new templates, smearing them with grape honey, I'll
challenge you for the right to beleaguer. To which he assented
abstractedly and it was over in a thrush. Not to . . . well excuse me
too. Curses I'd already signed on,

there was no need to jump for it, put a good face on it. Mild eyes
expressing a child's dignity. OK for it to rot, it
was pompous to begin with.

"No, don't hang him," says he, for he killed a hare yesterday. And if you
don't believe me I'll show you the hare alive in a basket.

So they built a pontoon bridge, and when they had crossed over the fish applauded.
I was aghast, lost forty pounds at the gaming tables of the
Channel Islands, 'sblood I said. So I set fire to my bow, poised my arrow,
and shot amongst them. I broke seventeen ribs on one side,
and twenty-one and a half on the other; but my arrow passed clean through
without ever touching it, and the worst was I lost my arrow;

however I found it again in the hollow of a tree. I felt it; it felt
clammy. I smelt it; it smelt honey.

We were warned about spiders, and the occasional famine.
We drove downtown to see our neighbors. None of them were home.
We nestled in yards the municipality had created,
reminisced about other, different places—
but were they? Hadn't we known it all before?

In vineyards where the bee's hymn drowns the monotony,
we slept for peace, joining in the great run.
He came up to me.
It was all as it had been,
except for the weight of the present,
that scuttled the pact we made with heaven.
In truth there was no cause for rejoicing,
nor need to turn around, either.
We were lost just by standing,
listening to the hum of wires overhead.

We mourned that meritocracy which, wildly vibrant,
had kept food on the table and milk in the glass.
In skid-row, slapdash style
we walked back to the original rock crystal he had become,
all concern, all fears for us.
We went down gently
to the bottom-most step. There you can grieve and breathe,
rinse your possessions in the chilly spring.
Only beware the bears and wolves that frequent it
and the shadow that comes when you expect dawn.

DAYS OF RECKONING

Questions about the timing
intruded. The last client
before dawn was seen at a certain
distance. Then they brought up

the whole other issue of belonging.
Seems we weren't welcome despite
having occupied Hollyhock House
for generations upon generations.

Then a more remote client raised "issues"
closer to one, like a warm breeze from the cape,
seen to oscillate in an argument—
vexed particles. The captain was really sad

about that one. He came selling articles
door to door, from time to time. A personage
much beloved and little thought of.
He'd bought his first perimeter

with a baby tooth at the age of six.
Afterwards, when they asked him how he felt
about it, he was evasive, but in a way
that charmed every hearer. Dogs knew him

as a faithful friend, and tinkers
always had a stray dam for him.
Growing up lively in the house,
his ears soon pierced its roof.

[. . .]

At sixteen he attended his first dance,
met the charming Miss Letty.
There was another claimant, elusive,
predatory, veering to elvish embroilment

when the territories were divvied up at last.
The maid sent to say they could come down
if a clean breast were to be made of it.
As happened, that very evening, as I and others

can attest. The captain looked spiffy in his garb.
Rubies lurked in beads of lamplight, the joint
was carved and tears washed down with wine
whose bitter taste endures to this day.

That meant that these cocktails became more and more pointed at the situation of the masses—at Edie, at Mrs. Pogarski, at the space between her legs, at von Klunk. So the snowball got lost up ahead. It had succeeded in its mission, which was to put everybody out of doors for fifteen minutes. When they returned it was as though to a later act of the shabby costume drama in which all had become embedded like La Brea tar. There were new solutions wiggling to be applied and old ones which had been superseded though they lived on in the public consciousness like the memory of a beloved opera star and her tresses in a cell in the walls of an alveolate neo-gothic parlor. Fears that the snowball had reached extinction, or that it had been fatally sidetracked in the Coma Berenices of its own perverse self-projection through the dangerous daydreams of housewives, their hands at rest in the dishwater of a kitchen sink, or retirees and empty-nesters wishing to refinance the mortgage on their house or move to a smaller one or rent out part of it, proved premature. What piquantly captured the imagination of each, from competitor to consumer to straw boss to newly outsourced consultant, was how all-inclusive the bench warrant was. No beating about the bed of roses here!

Edie had felt vaguely apprehensive since the afternoon a dark-hatted man had called while she was out. He had said something about testing the water, her maid Maria told her. There had never been a problem with the water before. Maybe it was part of some ruse to get into the house and rummage around in Carl's papers. He hadn't called or returned. Yet she was left with the fact that he *had* been there; that something or someone wanted part of her attention; that is to say, part of her.

At five o'clock she mixed cocktails—for herself and Carl, should he show up—in the shaker old Mrs. Lavergne had left her. Bombay Sapphire martinis. Carl had fallen in love with them in Bangalore where he had been posted on an assignment. Somehow it was always a disappointment when they came out of the shaker colorless instead of blue. The sapphire color was in the bottle. She wondered if Carl had noticed this, or, more important, whether it bothered him. He had been so tight-lipped lately—though always the affectionate dear he had been on the day they first met at the Cayuga Country Club. Well, he'd had a lot on his mind. The refinancing hadn't been going too well—at least that was her impression, since he hadn't talked about it. When things went well he grew expansive, his tone avuncular. "Well, let's see what the pixies left in the larder last night. Maybe some little cheesie-biskies?"

The battlefront heat had been singeing everybody's nerves. Maria, badly off, had complained of backache. The arcane arousing had taken place on schedule. Then the arraignment was ascendant. The executive expectation, expecting expression, expectorated artwork, i.e., visual arts. The work of art had not arrived.

"Cut the mustard, curvaceous. This cutthroat-dance can't continue forever. I was downtown, saw your image enthroned above the city, through the grille, dilatory; apes and aphids continued pouring into the place. Soon we'll be looking at calmer quarters, a jar of moonshine reflecting the moon as in days gone by." Those were my sentiments too. Alas, Edie, we are no longer ourselves. Something came by and cut me down in the night. I was sure you'd notice. But the next day and the day after that came and went, and after that it was uncertain whether the observatory octet had finished chiming beneath the liquid dome. We were all to blame. Collective guilt is the only sure bet. But now I want you weaving in and out of my letter to the editor, dated tomorrow. A Coromandel screen has patience only with itself, but a quaff of grappa sees into and pierces the region of near mists we know we know how to deal with.

The snowball is a model for the soul because billions of souls are embedded in it, though none can dominate or even characterize it. In this the snowball is like the humblest soul that ever walked the earth. The rapacious, the raw, are its satellites. It wants you to believe its core is the outermost shell of the universe, which may or may not be true. Each of us has the choice of believing it, but we cannot believe in both things without becoming separated from our core of enigma, which soldiers on in good times and bad, protecting us alike from the consequences of inaction and misguided enthusiasm. The snowball would melt before it would release us from our vows.

After a mostly painful few years spent in Moscow (Idaho!), we changed to Illinois. At first the cultural advantages of living in a large university town were a boon, after the isolation we'd experienced. But gradually harsher realities began to make themselves felt. A French film, an evening at the ballet or a concert (mostly symphonic warhorses, like the 1812 Overture) every couple of months were hardly sufficient to keep reflections on what we were missing out on in the big city from showing through the threadbare drapes of our lives. The satin roof of our Colonial Revival house looked fine from the street, but when you were under it you felt crushed by the weight of the old twentieth century. The college radio station emitted a perpetual flood of oldies or post-Schoenbergian twangs. Even the book discussions ("round tables") seemed mostly aimed at a "young adult" audience. Mind you, neither Stu nor I have anything against the younger generation—we're not that far from it ourselves, kind of at the tail end of the baby-boom era. But so much serious attention brought to bear on subjects of doubtful consequence can get to you after a while. Many's the time we'd stare at each other across the living room and wonder, "So what?" Then one day a remarkable change occurred.

Some of us, quite a few, were fettered, many were not. The topiary Trojan horse stood outside the gate, not wanting to be let in. The free-lance were blue; the staff yellow. A stiff breeze was gathering itself in the west, indifferent to those who lay magnetized in its path or scurried to find some primitive shelter, a hollow log or overturned canoe. Jarvis and April, up to their necks in mimosa, could have cared less what intentions had etched themselves into the gigantic forehead that now loomed over all. A shrill fragrance, too aromatic for some, stood in the forward fields. I am benison, it sang; others may take heed or go back to their status as prisoners. But we, we all, are the stuff of legends, we urged. A quiet space for bathing, adorable beds that chase you into sleep, for dinner a dish of boiled puffin's eggs. Be careful, you'll disturb the pests, er, pets, April breathed. And if a few of them were released in time for tomorrow's match? Go, suffer with them. The carnage, the pandemonium go at it, as is their custom. Downstairs an old servant lurks, indifferent to minute changes in the wallpaper pattern, our unique heritage.

Today was nicer for a change. Marnie and Val are on their way to a trip through the New England states. In August, Merle stopped by "just to visit." We went to the new fish place and it was good. In February the two boys took me to the figure skating championships in Cincinnati, which I try never to miss. A month later we scrambled along the Carolina coast hoping for signs of spring. They were few and far between, mostly redbuds in bloom.

Not a particularly attractive flower but one is grateful for any little swatch of color at that time of year. In late April and May the season kind of bottomed out. Too much rain. Evidence of copulation everywhere. I'm sure I missed a lot of the usual flowers of the spring, destroyed by the eccentric weather. At such times staying home can be a real blessing.

Summer was quiet except for the usual "transients." Fran and Don stopped by on their way to the traditional games in the Scottish highlands. They are centuries old and an amazing sight, it seems. Each sent a card from Scotland. Mary and her little boy came by in August. We went to the fish place but I'm not sure if Lance (her boy) appreciated it. Children have such pronounced tastes and can be quite stubborn about it. In late September a high point was the autumn foliage which was magnificent this year. Casper took me and his wife's two aunts on a "leaf-peeping" trip in northern Vermont. We were near Canada but didn't actually cross the border. You can get the same souvenir junk on this side for less money Max said. He is such a card.

November. Grief over Nancy Smith.

All in all this has been a fairly active and satisfying year, and I'm looking forward to the next one. Where it will take me I do not know. I just hang on and try to enjoy the ride. Snow brings winter memories. There is a warning somewhere in this but I do not know if it will be transmitted.

THE NEW HIGHER

You meant more than life to me. I lived through
you not knowing, not knowing I was living.
I learned that you called for me. I came to where
you were living, up a stair. There was no one there.
No one to appreciate me. The legality of it
upset a chair. Many times to celebrate
we were called together and where
we had been there was nothing there,
nothing that is anywhere. We passed obliquely,
leaving no stare. When the sun was done muttering,
in an optimistic way, it was time to leave that there.

Blithely passing in and out of where, blushing shyly
at the tag on the overcoat near the window where
the outside crept away, I put aside the there and now.
Now it was time to stumble anew,
blacking out when time came in the window.
There was not much of it left.
I laughed and put my hands shyly
across your eyes. Can you see now?
Yes I can see I am only in the where
where the blossoming stream takes off, under your window.
Go presently you said. Go from my window.
I am half in love with your window I cannot undermine
it, I said.

Newfoundland is, or was, full of interesting people.
Like Larry, who would make a fool of himself on street corners
for a nickel. There was the Russian who called himself
the Grand Duke, and who was said to be a real duke from somewhere,
and the woman who frequently accompanied him on his rounds.
Doc Hanks, the sawbones, was a real good surgeon
when he wasn't completely drunk, which was most of the time.
When only half drunk he could perform decent cranial surgery.
There was the blind man who never said anything
but produced spectral sounds on a musical saw.

There was Walsh's, with its fancy grocery department.
What a treat when Mother or Father
would take us down there, skidding over slippery snow
and ice, to be rewarded with a rare fig from somewhere.
They had teas from every country you could imagine
and hard little cakes from Scotland, rare sherries
and Madeiras to reward the aunts and uncles who came dancing.
On summer evenings in the eternal light it was a joy
just to be there and think. We took long rides
into the countryside, but were always stopped by some bog or other.
Then it was time to return home, which was OK with everybody,
each of them having discovered he or she could use a little shuteye.

In short there was a higher per capita percentage of interesting people
there than almost anywhere on earth, but the population was small,
which meant not too many interesting people. But for all that
we loved each other and had interesting times
picking each other's brain and drying nets on the wooden docks.
Always some more of us would come along. It is in the place
in the world in complete beauty, as none can gainsay,
I declare, and strong frontiers to collide with.

Worship of the chthonic powers may well happen there
but is seldom in evidence. We loved that too,
as we were a part of all that happened there, the evil and the good
and all the shades in between, happy to pipe up at roll call
or compete in the spelling bees. It was too much of a good thing
but at least it's over now. They are making a pageant out of it,
one of them told me. It's coming to a theater near you.

RETRO

It's really quite a thrill
when the moon rises above the hill
and you've gotten over someone
salty and mercurial, the only person you ever loved.

Walks in the park are enjoyed.
Going to Jerusalem now
I walked into a hotel room.
I didn't need a name or anything.
I went to Bellevue Hospital,
got a piece of the guy.
As I say, it's really quite a thrill.

Quite a thrill too to bend objects
that always return to their appointed grooves—
will it be always thus? Or will auto parts
get to have their day in the sun?

Got to drone now.
Princess Ida plans to overwork us four days a week
until the bracts have mauved up.
Then it's a tailgate party—
how would you like your burger done?

A little tea with that?

I saw her wailing for some animals.
That doesn't mean a thing doesn't happen
or only goes away, or gets worse.
What's the worst that could happen?

[. . .]

The midnight forest drags you along, thousands of peach hectares. Told him I wouldn't do it if I was him. Nothing to halt the chatter of locusts until they're put away for the night. He edges closer to your locker. Why did I leave it open? I've forgotten the combination. But it seems he's not interested in the locker, maybe my shoe—something unlike anything he's ever known. Sensing the tension he broke the ice with a quip about the weather somewhere, or maybe—maybe an observation on time, how it moves vastly in different channels, always keeping up with itself, until the day—I'm going to drive back to the office, a fellowship of miles, collect some of last year's ammunition. Then I'm definitely going to the country, he laughs.

ANNUALS AND PERENNIALS

Telling it so simple, so far away,
as this America, home of the free,
colored ashes smeared on the base
or pedestal that flourishes ways of doubting
to be graceful, wave a slender hand . . .

We are fleet and persecuting
as hawks or crows.
We suffer for the lies we told, not wanting to
yet cupped in the wristlock of grace,
teenage Borgias or Gonzagas,
gold against gray in bands streaming,
meaning no harm, we never

meant it to, this stream that outpours now
haplessly into the vestibule that awaits.

We have shapes but no power.

HEAVY HOME

. . . hungry eaters of a slender substance
—C. M. DOUGHTY

One thing follows another awning in the event horizon. One life in the going changes the subject. Some things made sense, others didn't. I didn't expect to die so soon. Well, I guess I'll have to have tabulated myself in some way. I'd discussed writing on your leg. Others in the tree school groaned, stirred in their sleep, having lately put away childish things. All of us late. What if we lived overseas? We could survive on alms and pledges for a while, find jobs in the barrel industry, decoct melismas on which to build an echo.

Here we break camp; it was decreed by an elder, or alder. He put the water on to boil. He sends us itches and the wherewithal to scratch them, fossils in the guise of party favors. Then sprang dull-headed into the gilded surround, chimera after all. Tears from the doll leaked out. It was as if we had chosen this path on a different journey, and were waiting in the deafening wilderness for our instincts to catch up, leggy hope.

Many flushings of the toilet later you'll give it back and we'll give it to the mechanical oracle, render unto caesura, and expect thrifty thanks, somewhere between laughter and obloquy. But how quaint the semicircular drive and its trimmings: gazing globe, lark's mirror, lime twigs, tinsel, ormolu, Venus's-flytrap, *pattes de velours*, Rembrandt and his goat. On a return visit we were not received, the grace period having expired.

The pictograph is also a chimera. Since day one you've abused it. Resting on our oars we breathe in the attar of dissent, breaking off of negotiations, recall of ambassadors, the rift within the lute. For the time being the disputed enclave is yours. But its cadence is elsewhere.

THE TEMPLATE

was always there, its existence seldom
questioned or suspected. The poets of the future
would avoid it, as we had. An imaginary railing
disappeared into the forest. It was here that the old gang
used to gather and swap stories. It
was like the Amazon, but on a much smaller scale.

Afterwards, when some of us swept out into the world
and could make comparisons, the fuss seemed justified.
No two poets ever agreed on anything, and that amused us.
It seemed good, the clotted darkness that came every day.

THE SNOW-STAINED PETALS AREN'T
PRETTY ANY MORE

A chance encounter in the street, an ancient phrase offered by a delicate woman, sends him back to burrow in the rubble of his youth. A few viable wisps still protrude. It all involves fetishes, those poor misunderstood employees of the sexual closet. Despised worker bees. Those bondsmen are in town, bonding. And what shall I tell the sales representative when he calls? That we don't need any fireworks. We're living backward. We're not making up for the mistakes of the past, we are the past.

He was sinking into a kind of lethargic kick the house had never seen him in. And was hiding in one. You, always so good at the old days when something you do for the young ladies comes up again in conversation, can you still conjugate? The gray parrot stretches his alarming scarlet wing, and the room falls silent, save for the hastily indrawn breath of a few of the participants. It's four o'clock, you've come late, that wraps up nap time. The old fake dilemma, not urgent. I've even forgotten it, so go on with your story. Man walks into bar. Stilled avalanches back up, in slow motion. White snow on dun cement. For the seasons to withdraw, cherries must first come alive, in a burst of somewhat embarrassing frankness, while the distant rumble goes on: the opportunity for something to do something else, for it to be something else. Meanwhile, the Hardys ride high. Why? They didn't send the blotch to me, the postmark is missing. And the stamp? All colliding, twisting like train smoke in the wind, rattled by the elements. To punish people after dark. Buster issued a warning. In the shape of a message in a bottle, cast into the sea off the Cape of Good Hope. When his sister found it some twelve years later all his prognostications had come true, yet they hadn't mattered much. No one had paid attention. Such, my friends, is the reward of study and laborious attempts to communicate with the dead. In the end it all falls to pieces.

SONNET: MORE OF SAME

Try to avoid the pattern that has been avoided,
the avoidance pattern. It's not as easy as it looks:
The herringbone is floating eagerly up
from the herring to become parquet. Or whatever suits it.
New fractals clamor to be identical
to their sisters. Half of them succeed. The others
go on to be Provençal floral prints some sleepy but ingenious
weaver created halfway through the eighteenth century,
and they never came to life until now.

It's like practicing a scale: at once different and never the same.
Ask not why we do these things. Ask why we find them meaningful.
Ask the cuckoo transfixed in mid-flight
between the pagoda and the hermit's rococo cave. He may tell you.

THE LOVE INTEREST

We could see it coming from forever,
then it was simply here, parallel
to the day's walking. By then it was we
who had disappeared, into the tunnel of a book.

Rising late at night, we join the current
of tomorrow's news. Why not? Unlike
some others, we haven't anything to ask for
or borrow. We're just pieces of solid geometry:

cylinders or rhomboids. A certain satisfaction
has been granted us. Sure, we keep coming back
for more—that's part of the "human" aspect
of the parade. And there are darker regions

penciled in, that we should explore some time.
For now it's enough that this day is over.
It brought its load of freshness, dropped it off
and left. As for us, we're still here, aren't we?

COMPOSITION

We used to call it the boob tube,
but I guess they don't use tubes anymore.
Whatever, it serves a small purpose after waking
and before falling asleep. Today's news—
but is there such a thing as news,
or even oral history? Yes, when you want to go back
after a while and appraise the accumulation
of leaves, say in a sandbox.
The rest is rented depression,
available only in season
and the season is always next month,
a pure but troubled time.

That's why I don't go out much, though
staying at home never seemed much of an option.
And speaking of nutty concepts, surely "home"
is way up there on the list. I feel more certain about "now"
and "then," because they are close to me,
like lovers, though apparently not in love with me,
as I am with them. I like to call to them,
and sometimes they reply, out of the deep business of some dream.

Shifting, too anxious to be fully aware, the screen of dirt and glitter grazes the edge of the pavement. It is understood that this is now the past, sixty, sixty-four years ago. It matters precisely at the drip of blood forming at the end of an icicle that hisses at you, you're a pod of a man. You know, forget and dislike him.

The row of dishes stretched into the distance, dreaming. Is it Japan where you are? Who are these slate prisons, aligned, half bowing offstage, half erupting out of the prompter's box? Glycerin stains the cheeks

and the old fire tongs have their say. This is a story in a chest. Conversations at night not meant to be overheard, so you can't tell exactly when you came in, at which second. The interior is meant to be homey upstairs, downstairs, all across the hall, dazzled from the blue microsecond it took to get here, but if then, why? Why the commotion on the shore? Traces of birds in the sand, birdshit, claw marks. And the rest are missing.

Soon bread will announce itself. To be seen from behind, here is what you have to do. Smear a tongue depressor with a little suet, then stand away, pessimistic as always. The part in your hair will come to seem the natural one. Your faded red T-shirt is indeed ours to look at. Except there are too many middle-aged rubes now. You know, you've got to go out, jostle the barometer, bump into the hall tree and excuse yourself, descend three steps, walk to the curb and pee against someone's sedan. Then it may turn out that you have seen *your* back. A joyful roar lit up the headlands, from afar

screeching white as the World's Columbian Exposition, inspiration to architects of the burgeoning Twentieth Century, swarming now, too hungry to appease, let's get on with it. But you have to do it more often. To qualify for some of that relief aid. Kings in their dungeons applaud the new centennial, McKinley assassinated. Lake Erie broods, pushes its lower lip out. OK, if you can get all you want through mismanagement, this late-breaking trust buster can do the same, providing you all shape up. Mansions and fac-tories line Dakota Boulevard. Skyboards, and the dark rhythms of houses, shuttered, for-ever, what concept is that? In the end the jazz reaches will effort it out. Darn it,

[. . .]

I like your lingo. We two be here all the same. The Russian sparrows wheel pesteringly, no it is not time to come in, I said no it is not a time to come in. Fine we'll stay out where it's mild,

contingency is all the rage here. I said . . . No but there comes a time when contingency itself is contingent on the abrupt desire to happen, a colossal burp brewing somewhere. And moreover what I maintained to you once stands, signpost in the desert pointing the wrong way, we'll get back whatever way we can, sure as heck. Then you just came around the barn's edge as though materializing, it wouldn't have taken much. So why didn't I . . . didn't we . . . It's past time, half past time, too late but another time, so long, so long for a while, geez I don't know, the answer, if I did, you—and if I did . . .

Effably, it talks on, not paring it, scrambled then restructured, a song to remember in reckless sleep, bygones. She used to say, "as Amy would say, as Leon would say," and let this stand as a portal cut into the granite face, from which one could view shards within, boulders tormented as though by torrents, but still, as though motion had never dreamed of sleep. Then to stand up and stretch, the day draining. Scratch any itch, the somber legato underneath will surge prominently, lean on the right lever. Absence

relieves itself, got to be getting on with those notes. Let's see . . . Wherever a tisket is available, substitute an item from column B, then return to the starting goal. The challenger barely had time to mouth our initials, the glaze was off the cake, whoa, before there were few but now they are all of a piece, snoring to drown the freesia's reticence. Charles is gone. He used to live here, when blood erupted into riots and the frugal demurrers retreated all of a sudden. We like to use to be here, scrubbing soap stone, celebrating rags in my head to make the antlers glow. Use medium strength bleach until pursued clobbered effect pulsates in little burrs, grace notes in an awful cataract, groans we anticipated, revelers' premature hoo-ha. Grouchy he acceded, a jobber's whisk

parses the banished interval. But why talk of housebreaking on a night like this? To one viewer, off in different directions with elaborate casualness, to regroup behind Rusty's garage, concocting who knows what deviltry, having conveniently evaporated from the hoary scribe's all-consuming minutes. And if you were to tape the *remous* famously issuing from the ensuing gaggle—would you do it differently? For time, and this is where it gets really nasty, remembers all of us, recognizes us making allowances for our changed appearance and greets us familiarly by name, only occasionally getting mixed up (though it does happen). So who's to blame us for signing off on our agenda and sinking into a cozy chair, accepting the proffered sherry and sighing for a time when things really were easier and more people were alive. That, and Jack's tattoo. But there was something else slinking up via the back way and mingling with the invited guests, *mine de rien*. Not a bailiff or a rejected suitor from prelapsarian school picnics, nor yet a seemingly indifferent observer, tie-clasp camera getting it all down, nor a truly open-minded member of the cultivated bourgeoisie our grandfathers sprang from or knew about, but a cosmic dunce, bent on mischief and good works with equal zest, somebody fully determined to *be* and not disturb others with his passive-aggressive version of how things are and ever shall be—the distinguished visiting lecturer.

Smack in the limousine, the friendly fog next door placed a hand on my shoulder, cementing matters. The professor looked wary. "Flowers have helped pave roads," he mooted. The ocean filling in for us. Too many vacant noon empires, without them you can't rule a hemisphere or be sated other than by watching. Our TV brains sit around us all brave and friendly, like docile pets. We get by by tweaking. Seems it's always going on in another's head, far from the painted asters and the glorious headlands of Maine, far from everything you could just about entertain. Was that you sermonizing? Go right ahead, be my guest. I'll sit here in the blue room till it's time, cradling my wrists in my shawl. But I wish to be remembered, if only by you. Make it stick.

Oh, *that* traveling salesman. And, enthused, I bought away from the long procession of vowels in pajamas. It was as though I and the world didn't matter. And thick the birds plowed the air, as though driven by an intimate force like that which animates the Ouija board. Did I say that? Yes, that's what the man said beholden to the garlands of woven fruit and beribboned cartouches, amen. What we have here are certain individuals intent on disarraying the public gravitas of things. Others, threadbare acolytes in the slow-moving sift of moulting opinion as it degrades to a screen behind which a nordic lake escapes upwards into ecstatic pastures, demur. But we began by positing the structural integrity of vapor, now it's hysteria twice over, once round the bend and two's your fancy, whatever it chooses to reveal of itself. And that is more than you get studying in a school, observing rain as it enters the rainbarrel. To think it was you that only yesterday protested the convenience of the loom's double keyboard. Now you seem launched in your own narrative, in memory's despite. The vast memorial due here fumbles its own branching hee-haw. For shame to lie like that, and over lunch. Well, it *is* due, and that's what can be said for it. I'll posit your binding resolution in the day after tomorrow's brush with de-definition. For now all bets are off.

The president always knew, under her lilacs was a liver fading. Yes, I can think of a number of things which would surprise you if you knew the soundtrack. Heterophage, we come unblinking into the standing day and tool off in several directions once our duties are accomplished. Guarding the kids, throwing junk into the adjacent yard. Sometimes the silent backup slops over the fountain's edge, and then it's a race to the unfulfilled spaces that are still blanks on the city's grid. The guardians of our tacit belonging are stilled then, we err on the sidelines and mope. The delusion comes undone with a roar. We think we have an appointment with a snowman, so is it written anyway in our date-book. But the guy just left, headed for warmer climes. And thus the breathtaking precision of our off moments drifts down the vacant plaque and its reeded copper surround. Weren't we supposed to be taking note of the new eldritch morphing into a chromatic classicism whose contour trembles like mercury, eager to be taken aboard? Alas for our foreshadowing,

for though we wander like lilies, there are none that can placate us, or not at this time. Originally we were meant as a backdrop for "civilization," the buses and taxis splurging along ring roads, anxious to please customers, though the latter proved to be in short supply. Like so many figure-ground dilemmas, this was resolved with moderately pleasing results for all concerned. Time's *arrière-pensée* floats down from on high, settles near our ankles, confirming our brush with whatever. The ensuing uproar allows us to take French leave of the other swiftly departing guests, to achieve maximum freshness once the door has closed and the great caesura of the sky, twitching with stars, fixes its noncommittal gaze on us, enabling us to stand erect and inhale huge gusts of astringent air. We are aware that we are doing something and are thus prepared to follow the event's traces as far as need be, beyond the sea and the mountains and the ridgepole at the world's end and the attendant generations.

Abruptly the season backed up. Bright green out of the red. Almost fell off my empire. On recent to-ing and fro-ing, the same old same old, the record is silent, save in vertical chirps, amounting at times to a carol, or motet. The little bomb works, it seems. Now that's one for the record books, us salivating an eternity till the sun goes down in an outer husk of our hemisphere. But a virtual contest is all it ever gets up to. A mirror shipped from halfway around the world records the whisper that begat its strangely impersonal voyage into the lap of the present, my stagger of inattention and the consequent drumroll. Invading the privacy of millions with a lurid bedtime story, the little dog laughs, climbs the stepstool bearing red carnations and lapses. The laughter begins slowly at the bottom of the orchestra pit and wells gradually toward the back; it seems to say it's OK not to be counted, you'll belong eventually even if you're not wearing the right armband or redingote. I crawled through a culvert to get here and you're right to love me, I was only a little awry, now it's my fancy to be here and with you, alright, fluted, not toxic. Prepare the traditional surprise banquet of braised goat.

You wore your cummerbund with the stars and stripes. I, kilted in lime, held a stethoscope to the head of the parting guest. Together we were a couple forever.

INDEX OF TITLES AND FIRST LINES

[End-of-line punctuation in each first line is retained as it appears in the original poem; ellipses indicate a continuing line of a prose poem.]